CARLA HEGEMAN CRIM

ESSENTIAL
Sewing
Reference TOOL

- All-in-One Visual Guide
- Tools & Supplies
- Stitches & Se...
- Ruffles & Bia...
- Zippers & Bu...
- Sewn Access...
- Home Dec • Garment Making
- Sizing Charts for All Ages
- & More!

stashBOOKS®
an imprint of C&T Publishing

D1466036

Publisher: Amy Marson

Creative Director: Gailen Runge

Art Director/Book Designer:
Kristy Zacharias

Editor: Liz Aneloski

Technical Editors: Doreen Hazel,
Teresa Stroin, and Ann Haley

Production Coordinator: Rue Flaherty

Production Editor: Joanna Burgarino

Illustrator: Mary E. Flynn

Photo Assistant: Mary Peyton Peppo

Cover photography by Nissa Brehmer;
Instructional photography by Diane
Pedersen, unless otherwise noted

Published by Stash Books, an imprint of C&T Publishing, Inc.,
P.O. Box 1456, Lafayette, CA 94549

Library of Congress Cataloging-in-Publication Data

Crim, Carla Hegeman.

 Essential sewing reference tool : all-in-one visual guide - tools & supplies - stitches & seam treatments - ruffles & bias tape - zippers & buttonholes - sewn accessories - home dec - garment making - sizing charts for all ages - & more! / Carla Hegeman Crim.

    pages cm

 Includes index.

  ISBN 978-1-60705-860-1 (soft cover)

 1. Sewing. I. Title.

 TT705.T775 2014

 646.2--dc23

 2013024144

 Printed in China

 10 9 8 7 6 5 4 3 2 1

Contents

Sewing Machines

BASIC MECHANICAL SEWING MACHINE

Simple, motorized machine that makes straight, zigzag, and usually a few decorative stitches. Stitch settings are controlled manually with knobs.

COMPUTERIZED SEWING MACHINE

Makes a wide variety of utility and decorative stitches. Stitch settings are controlled by buttons or a touch screen that is connected to an internal computer chip.

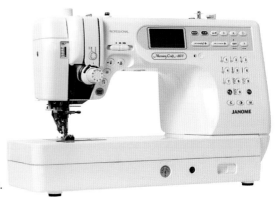

EMBROIDERY MACHINE

Stitches digitized embroidery design files. It can be a stand-alone machine or a module that works in combination with a computerized machine.

QUILTING MACHINE

Features a larger work area and more advanced feeding mechanisms than a standard computerized machine.

OVERLOCK MACHINE

Also known as a serger. Utilizes multiple threads to simultaneously stitch and finish seams. Features include a blade for trimming edges prior to stitching and a stitch finger for creating rolled hems.

Sewing Machine Feet

STANDARD FEET

For general stitching

FOOT	FEATURES/PURPOSE
Straight-stitch	Exclusively for straight stitching. Gives even pressure for fine or thick fabrics.
Zigzag-stitch	All-purpose foot for straight stitching, zigzag stitching, and most decorative stitches. Allows for needle position adjustment.
Zipper	Open on one or both sides to allow for variable needle placement and stitching close to zipper coils or bulky embellishments.

Photos on pages 7–9 courtesy of BERNINA of America

FLANGED FEET

Feature thin, smooth blades called flanges that act as guides for stitching placement.

FOOT	FEATURES/PURPOSE
Blind-hem	Aligns with a fold, so the appropriate stitch barely catches the fabric (see Machine Blindstitched Hem, page 30).
¼″ piecing	Sews a perfect ¼″ from the raw edge with a right side flange on the outside of the foot to maintain the ¼″ seam. On the inside of the foot a notch is cut out as a guide for ⅛″ seams.
Edgestitching	Allows for precise edgestitching, topstitching, and in-the-ditch stitching.
Overcast	Gives a clean edge finish on most fabrics. Especially good for knit fabrics that tend to curl on the edges.

GROOVED FEET

Facilitate centered passage of trims and thick specialty stitches.

FOOT	FEATURES/PURPOSE
Open-toe or Satin-stitch	Wide passage allows for more visibility and flexibility than a standard foot. The groove on the bottom accommodates a thicker stitch mound.
Pin-tuck	Works in conjunction with a twin needle to make raised tucks in the fabric.
Cording	For centered attachment of one or more cords or thin trims.
Piping	For side or centered attachment of thicker trims such as piping, gimp, and pearls.
Invisible-zipper	Gives precise stitching placement for installation of invisible zippers.

BUTTONHOLING AND BUTTON-SEWING FEET

Designed to automatically make identical buttonholes (see One-Step Buttonholes, page 68), and to attach buttons by machine (see Tip: Attaching Buttons by Machine, page 70).

HEMMING AND RUFFLING FEET

Direct one or more layers of fabric into the proper position for stitching.

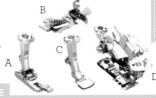

FOOT	FEATURES/PURPOSE
Rolled-hem (A)	Rolls the fabric edge into a narrow double-fold hem of a specified width.
Binding (B)	Equipped with a funnel that facilitates the wrapping and stitching of binding around the fabric edge.
Gathering (C)	Creates soft gathers in lightweight fabrics. The tightness of gathers is adjustable.
Ruffler attachment (D)	A moving blade tucks fabric during the stitching process and optionally attaches it to another fabric at the same time. Pleat depth and spacing are adjustable.

NONSTICK AND WALKING FEET

Allow for smooth sewing of sticky, shifty, thick, or otherwise challenging fabrics (such as leather, suede, velvet, and oilcloth).

FOOT	FEATURES/PURPOSE
Roller	"Wheels" on the bottom of the foot coast over the fabric.
Nonstick	Glides over plastic-coated fabrics such as oilcloth and laminated cotton.
Walking	Moves with the feed dog mechanism to evenly feed two or more layers of fabric through the machine.

FREE-MOTION FEET

Allow for user-controlled stitching with dropped feed dogs.

FOOT	FEATURES/PURPOSE
Darning	Used for simple back-and-forth stitching to repair holes. Also works for free-motion quilting.
Free-motion embroidery	Similar to the darning foot, but with an opening cut out for better needle visibility.

Cutting Tools

GENERAL SEWING SCISSORS

Ideal size and angle for snipping thread and fabric during the sewing process.

DRESSMAKER'S SHEARS

Large, heavy scissor angled for cutting out large pieces of fabric.

PINKING SHEARS

Large scissor with notched blades that produces nonfraying zigzag cuts.

APPLIQUÉ SCISSORS

Small, with a "duck bill" that acts as a guide for close cutting while protecting fabric.

THREAD SNIPS

Small spring-loaded clipper for quick, efficient thread snipping.

EMBROIDERY SCISSORS

Small, with sharp blades that fit into hard-to-reach areas to snip threads with precision.

ROTARY CUTTER

Circular blade that works in conjunction with a clear cutting ruler and a rotary cutting mat. Ideal for making straight cuts of fabric.

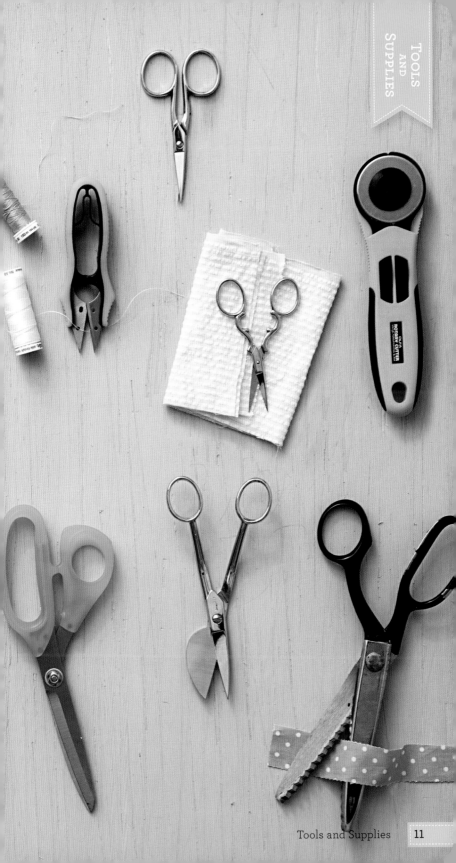

Pressing Tools

IRON AND IRONING BOARD

To smooth fabric and press seams during the sewing process.

SLEEVE BOARD

Small tabletop ironing board that fits into cylindrical shapes, such as sleeves, for crease-free pressing.

SEAM ROLL

Stuffed fabric roll similar to a sleeve board but smaller and more flexible. May also be wooden.

TAILOR'S HAM

Tightly stuffed fabric pillow with a wide end and a narrow end, used for pressing darts and curved seams.

PRESSING CLOTH

Placed over fabric while pressing to protect the fabric from the surface of the iron.

TEFLON PRESSING SHEET

Heat-resistant, nonstick material that allows for the application of double-sided fusible products to fabric. Also useful as a see-through pressing cloth.

Marking Tools

Follow manufacturer's directions when using removeable marking tools.

TOOL	ADVANTAGES	DISADVANTAGES
FABRIC MARKER	Makes clear and definite lines. Easy to use and remove.	Disappearing ink may fade too quickly or incompletely. Washable varieties may stain. Not suitable for darker fabrics.
FABRIC PENCIL	Makes crisp, water-soluble marks. Available in many colors.	Pressure needed to make marks may distort fabric. Marks not as bold as those made by markers.
TAILOR'S CHALK	Marks a wide variety of surfaces. Comes in solid, wheel, or pen forms.	Markings tend to rub or shake off with handling. Can dry out and become more difficult to use with age.
TRANSFER PAPER	Great for complex designs.	Paper tears easily. Markings are not as visible as other methods.

Sewing Machine Needles

Needle Size

Needle size is usually identified by two numbers: a top large number that is the shaft diameter in millimeters (European sizing) and a smaller bottom number that indicates standard U.S. sizing.

SIZES	RECOMMENDED FABRIC WEIGHTS AND EXAMPLES
60/8, 65/9, 70/10	Lightweight: Batiste, chiffon, crepe, fine linen, georgette, lamé, organdy, organza, rayon, satin, seersucker, silk, taffeta
75/11, 80/12, 90/14	Medium-weight: Broadcloth, corduroy, cotton (quilting), flannel, fleece, interlock, jersey, khaki, poplin, terry, wool
100/16, 110/18, 120/20	Heavyweight: Canvas, denim, faux fur, leather, oilcloth, thick wool, fabrics fused to heavy interfacing

Needle Type

Needle sharpness, silhouette, and eye shape are optimized for different fabrics and applications. General home sewing needles are designated by the letter H. A second letter may be assigned to denote the purpose and/or specific fabric.

TYPE	FEATURES/PURPOSE
Universal (H)	Slightly rounded point suitable for most woven, and some knit, fabrics.
Ball-point (H)	Rounded point for sewing knit fabrics such as jersey and interlock.
Stretch (H-S)	Rounded point for sewing elastic and highly stretchy knits. Designed to prevent skipped stitches.
Sharp (H-M)	Also called a microtex. The slim point is ideal for precision piecing and topstitching on most woven fabrics, especially microfiber fabrics.
Embroidery (H-E)	For decorative stitching and machine embroidery. Designed to protect delicate threads during rapid back-and-forth stitching motion.
Quilting (H-Q)	Tapered point for piecing and quilting multiple layers.
Denim (H-J)	Reinforced and shaped for thick or tightly woven fabrics, such as denim and heavy canvas.
Leather (H-LL)	Cutting point for leather and nonwoven synthetics.

Specialty Needles

Designed for specific stitches and threads, these needles include hem-stitch, top-stitch, and metallic needles. Twin and triple needles create rows of parallel stitching.

Straight Pins

All-purpose pins are sharp-pointed, about 0.6mm thick, and 1˝–2˝ long. Specialty pins vary in size and point style.

EXTRA FINE

For sheer or very delicate fabrics. Also called silk pins or satin pins.

BALL-POINT

Rounded tip specifically for knit fabrics

T-PIN

Thick, with a T-shaped head. For heavy fabrics such as upholstery.

APPLIQUÉ

Short and ideal for applying small trims and embellishments.

Pinhead style is mostly a matter of personal preference. Ball-shaped plastic heads are the most common, as they are easy to see and manipulate. Metal and glass heads are more heat-resistant. Flat plastic heads reduce bulk and distortion of fabric.

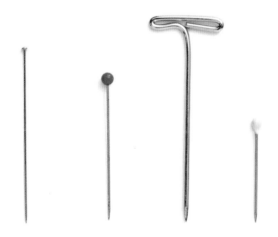

Thread

Thread Fiber Composition

Fiber content determines the stretchiness, sheen, and strength of the thread.

TYPE		FEATURES/PURPOSE
Natural	100% cotton	Matte luster and soft feel. For traditional sewing and quilting.
	Silk	High sheen and more elasticity than cotton. For decorative stitching and couture garment making.
Synthetic	Cotton-covered polyester	Good balance between strength and smooth finish. Suitable for all fabric types.
	100% polyester	Strong and economical, with medium luster. Suitable for most fabric types, including stretchy knits. Transparent form available.
	Rayon	High sheen. Ideal for machine embroidery.
	Nylon	Fluffy "woolly" form for stretch applications or embellishment. Transparent form for invisible stitching.
	Metallic	Nylon core coated with metal and polyester. For decorative stitching.

Thread Weight

Standard measuring system: the thicker the thread, the lower the weight designation.

	WEIGHT	FEATURES/APPLICATION
Relative Thickness	100	Very fine polyester or silk thread for nearly invisible stitching that sinks into and blends with the fabric.
	70	Cotton or transparent thread used in bobbins and heirloom sewing.
	60	Thin thread used in bobbins and for sewing thin fabrics.
	50	Fine thread popular for quilting and topstitching.
	40	Good balance of strength and delicate appearance. Standard weight for machine embroidery threads.
	30	General-purpose sewing thread.
	16–28	Thicker thread for upholstery, other heavyweight fabrics, and hand stitching.
	10–12	Heavy-duty thread for outdoor use, attaching buttons, and craft sewing.

Elastic

Elastic Fiber Content

Rubber or spandex is combined with a fiber to make elastic.

FIBER	FEATURES
Polyester	All-purpose, inexpensive, and withstands washing and dry-cleaning.
Cotton	Soft and traditional, but prone to shrinkage and not dry-cleanable.
Nylon	High sheen, delicate. Used mostly in swimwear and lingerie.

Elastic Type

The arrangement of the rubber strands and the fibers determines the stretch and strength of the elastic.

TYPE	FEATURES/APPLICATION
Woven	Strong and thick, retains width when stretched, and can be stitched without losing shape and elasticity. Good for heavy-duty applications.
Knit	Strong but lightweight and soft. Can be inserted into casings or directly stitched. Good for many garment applications.
Braided	Narrows when stretched for easy insertion into casings. Loses shape when stitched.

Elastic Style

Elastic comes in many styles, so choose the one that's right for your application.

TYPE	FEATURES/APPLICATION
Nonroll	Firm but thin. Does not curl. Perfect for waistbands.
Fold-over	Folds in half to bind and elasticize edges.
Buttonhole	Includes slits in the center to make adjustable waistbands.
Lingerie	Soft and light. Usually has a picot or lace edge for a feminine look.
Sport	Very soft. Includes channels for direct sewing to a waistband.
Clear	Made from solid polyurethane. Used for stabilizing knit seams.
Elastic thread	A core of rubber coated with a fiber. Can be wound onto a bobbin and used for shirring.

Other Notions

HAND SEWING NEEDLES

For fine finishing and embellishment.

NEEDLE	FEATURES/APPLICATION
Sharp	All-purpose medium-length sewing needle for general sewing.
Between	Short needle with a small eye for hand quilting.
Millinery	Long, thin needle for hat making, basting, and embroidery.
Embroidery	Similar to a sharp, but with a larger eye to accommodate embroidery floss.
Tapestry	Thicker needle with a large eye and blunt tip for needlework.
Darning	Long needle with a large eye and sharp point for mending and needlework.
Chenille	Thick needle with a large eye for needlework with thick yarn or threads, or silk ribbon work.
Upholstery	Thick straight or curved needle for heavy fabrics.

PINCUSHION

A small stuffed ball used for safe storage of pins, or a magnetized holder for picking up and storing pins.

THIMBLE

Protects finger when hand stitching. Made of plastic, metal, or leather.

SAFETY PINS

Hold layers together. Also used to pull elastics through casings and turn fabric tubes right side out.

SEAM RIPPER

Essential for removing misplaced seams or basting stitches. Also used to make slits in buttonholes.

BASTING TAPE

Double-stick tape that temporarily bonds fabric layers or attaches notions for accurate stitching.

MEASURING TOOLS

For obtaining accurate dimensions.

TOOL	APPLICATION
Clear ruler and cutting mat	Used with a rotary cutter to make straight cuts of fabric.
Yardstick	For measuring fabric yardage and other large linear items.
Tape measure	For measuring the human body and any other three-dimensional objects.
Flat hem gauge	Template for folding and pressing hems.
Sliding seam gauge	Short ruler for measuring and marking hems.

GLUESTICK

Temporarily holds fabrics or notions in place. Great for pockets, hook-and-loop tape, and zippers.

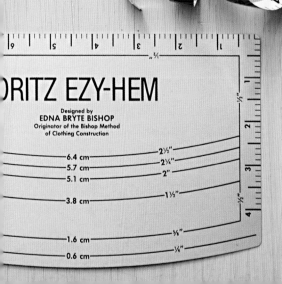

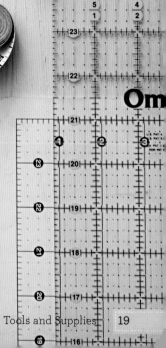

Stitches

Hand Sewing Stitches

STITCH	APPLICATION
Running stitch 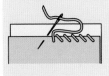	Basic piecing and embellishing.
Basting stitch 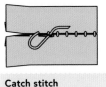	Temporarily holding pieces together for machine stitching.
Whipstitch 	For hemming. Invisible whipstitches catch only a few fibers of the outer fabric with the needle before reinsertion into the hem.
Slipstitch 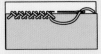	Stitching two folded, butted edges together.
Catch stitch	Hemming where a stretchy, durable stitch is required.
Backstitch	Joining heavy fabrics that require an extra-strong seam.
Blind hem stitch 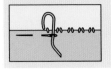	For hemming. Nearly invisible on the right side.

1. Insert a length of thread through the eye of the needle.

2. *For single-thread stitching*, tie a knot in one end and pull the thread so that the unknotted end is several inches away from the needle. *For double-thread stitching*, bring the ends together and tie a knot.

3. Insert the needle into the wrong side of the item and draw the thread through until the knot is at the insertion point.

4. Continue stitching and knot off at the end.

Machine Stitches

The stitch-length setting controls how far a single stitch travels. A small stitch length (1) gives tiny stitches, and a large stitch length (4–5) gives long stitches.

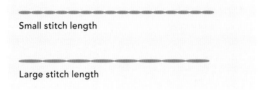

Small stitch length

Large stitch length

The stitch-width setting determines the side-to-side dimension of a stitch. Straight stitches have a width of 0, as there is no side-to-side movement. For a zigzag stitch, a small width setting (1) gives a narrow zigzag, and a large width setting (6–7) gives a wide zigzag.

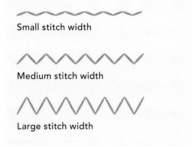

Small stitch width

Medium stitch width

Large stitch width

Stitch Tension

Most stitching is done with a mid-range, balanced tension setting. The needle thread tension can be adjusted for different fabrics and stitch types. A high-tension setting gives tight stitches that are strong but more prone to breakage or puckering. A low-tension setting gives loose stitches that are useful for basting or gathering. The bobbin thread tension is generally not adjusted unless there is a problem with the stitching.

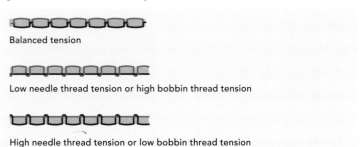

Balanced tension

Low needle thread tension or high bobbin thread tension

High needle thread tension or low bobbin thread tension

	STITCH		APPLICATION
BASIC MACHINE STITCHES	Straight stitch	-----------	General piecing, topstitching, and zippers. Long, loose stitches are used for basting and gathering.
	Zigzag stitch	∨∨∨∨	Edge finishing, stretch stitching, and appliqué. Satin stitches are made with a very short stitch-length setting.
	Tricot, or 3-step zigzag stitch	\/\/\/	Multipart zigzag stitch for topstitching and for edge finishing stretchy knit fabrics.
	Overcast stitch	∨∨∨∨	Stitch and edge finish seams simultaneously, much like a serger. Best used in conjunction with an overcast foot.
	Blind hem stitch	∧__∧__∧	Makes tiny stitches in the folded fabric to create nearly invisible stitching along a hem.
	Bridging or faggoting	∨∧∨∧	Joins two pieces of fabric at the edges. Used in heirloom sewing.
	Stretch stitch	≡≡≡≡≡≡≡:	Multistep straight stitch for sewing stretchy seams in highly elastic fabrics. Also used to reinforce seams.
	Decorative stitch		Embellishment or topstitching.

Seam Allowances

The distance between the stitching and the raw fabric edge depends on the type of seam and the need for adjustment.

Relative Seam Width

WIDTH	APPLICATION
⅝″	Common in home sewing patterns, this wide allowance gives room for "letting out" seams.
½″	Gives space for a wide finish, such as overlock machine stitches and French seams.
⅜″	Standard seam allowance in the garment industry (for minimal fabric waste). Gives some room for tailoring.
¼″	Preferred allowance for quilters. Also used in modern apparel patterns. Good for areas with curves or easing.
⅛″	Very small allowance that works only with nonfraying fabrics such as felt and leather. Wider allowances are often trimmed down to this size for better flexibility and reduced bulk.

Curved Seams

In quilting, this method is used to sew two curved pieces together within a two-dimensional design.

1. Fold the pieces in half to locate the centers. Mark the folds with pins.

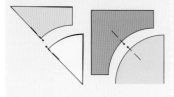

2. Match and pin the centers, with the right sides together and the convex piece on top.

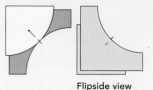

Flipside view

3. Match the corners at one end and pin.

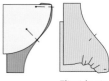

Flipside view

4. Align and pin the edges in between.

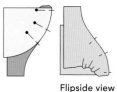

Flipside view

5. Repeat on the other side.

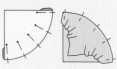

Flipside view

6. Stitch the curved pieces together with a ¼˝ seam, unless otherwise indicated. Use a straight stitch that is slightly longer than normal. Stitch slowly and use your fingertips to smooth out wrinkles as you go. Any puckers can be removed with a seam ripper and resewn.

7. Turn and press.

The matching process is similar to that of attaching a sleeve to a bodice in garment construction (page 106).

Simple Seam Finishes

Pinking

1. Stitch the seam with a ½″–⅝″ allowance (A).

2. Use pinking shears to trim the seam allowance down to ¼″–⅜″ (B).

3. Press open (B).

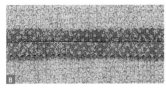

Straight Stitching

1. Stitch the seam with a ½″–⅝″ allowance.

2. Press open. Individually stitch each side of the seam allowance (A).

3. *Optional:* Add a second row of stitching parallel to the first (B).

4. Trim the raw edges with scissors or pinking shears, as desired. Press (C).

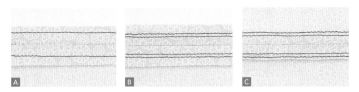

Straight Stitching and Folding

1. Stitch the seam with a ½″–⅝″ seam allowance. Press open.

2. Individually stitch each side of the seam allowance about ⅛″ from the raw edge (A).

3. Fold the raw edge under to meet the stitching from the original seam (B).

4. Individually stitch through the center of each folded seam allowance (C).

5. Press flat (D).

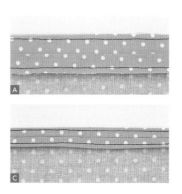

Overcasting

OPTION 1

1. Stitch the seam with a straight stitch.

2. Stitch the edges together with a zigzag, overcast, or overlock stitch.

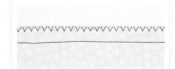

OPTION 2

1. Stitch the seam. Press open.

2. Stitch over each raw edge individually with a zigzag, overcast, or overlock stitch.

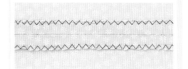

Couture Seam Finishes

Flat-Felled Seam

1. Stitch with a ½″–⅝″ seam allowance, right sides together. Press open (A).

2. Fold back the fabric on one side. Trim a side of the seam allowance to half of the original width (B).

3. Fold the wider allowance over the narrower allowance so that the raw edge is in line with the original seam stitching (C).

4. Open the fabrics and press the encased seam allowance to the side (D).

5. Stitch into place, very close to the folded edge (E).

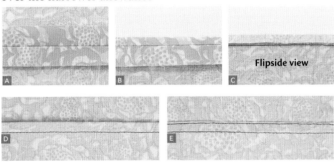

Flipside view

NOTE This seam can be started with the wrong sides of the fabric together, so that the fold ends up on the right side, adding detail to the garment.

French Seam

1. Start with clean, freshly cut edges with no fraying.

2. With the wrong sides together, stitch ⅛″ from the aligned edges (A).

3. Turn so that the right sides are facing each other. Press the seam with the stitching on the fold (B).

4. Stitch ⅜″ from the folded edge (C).

5. Press the seam to the side.

NOTE The resulting seam allowance is approximately ⅝″, so be sure to take this into account when cutting the fabric.

Hong Kong Finish

1. Cut 1¼˝-wide bias strips from a lightweight fabric (see Cutting and Joining Bias Strips, page 46).

2. Join the strips to create 2 bias strips long enough to encase both sides of the seam allowance.

3. With right sides together, stitch a ⅝˝ or wider seam. Press open (A).

4. Align a bias strip with one allowance edge and stitch with a ¼˝ seam (B).

5. Press the strip over and to the back of the allowance edge (C). Stitch in the ditch to secure (D).

6. From the underside, trim the bias strip close to the most recent stitching (E).

7. Repeat for the other side of the seam allowance (F).

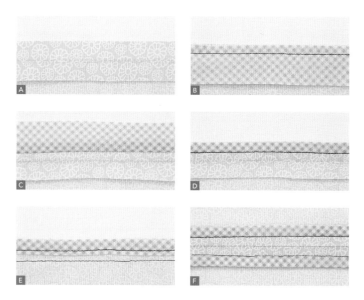

Hems

Single-Fold Hem

For best results, edge finish the raw edge of the hem allowance first (A). See Simple Seam Finishes, page 25.

1. Make a single fold of the desired length to the wrong side.

2. Hand or machine stitch into place (B).

Double-Fold Hem

1. Make a single fold about half the width of the hem allowance (A).

2. Make a second fold that is either the same size as, or a little wider than, the first fold.

3. Hand or machine stitch into place near the first folded edge (B).

Rolled Hem

1. Roll the edge of the fabric by hand or with a specialized machine foot (A).

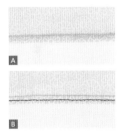

2. Sew a straight, zigzag, or overlock stitch to hold it in place (B).

Faced Hem

1. Align a separate strip of fabric with the raw edge, right sides together, and stitch into place (A).

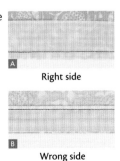

Right side

2. Turn the strip to the wrong side and press. Edge finish or fold under the strips's raw edge; then stitch into place (B).

Wrong side

Machine Blindstitched Hem

Many sewing machines have a blind hem stitch (page 22). The hem edge is folded like a fan and stitched so that the widest part of the blind hem stitch barely catches the edge of the fold (A). A blindstitch sewn by a machine is almost invisible on the outside of the garment (B). There are many books and online tutorials to guide beginners.

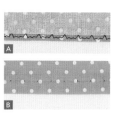

Hem Width

	WIDTH	APPLICATION
Relative Hem Width	Very wide (>2″)	A heavy hem gives the needed weight for draperies and long, full gowns. Also used in children's wear for clothing that can be "let out" with growth.
	Wide (1″–2″)	Often found in tailored dresses and pants. Allows a garment to hang properly without adding excessive weight.
	Medium (½″–¾″)	Common hem size for everything from knitwear to jeans. It is narrow enough to maneuver around tapers and flares and still hang nicely.
	Narrow (¼″–⅜″)	Works well with light- to medium-weight fabrics. Appropriate for shirttail hems and flowing blouses. Often found on home decor items such as napkins and tablecloths.
	Very narrow (<¼″)	Great for thin, sheer fabrics such as georgette and organza. Most often found in the form of a rolled hem made using a specialized machine foot.

Hemming Hints

HEMMING KNITS

When hemming knits, be sure to use a stitch that will stretch with the fabric. Zigzag and tricot stitches are inherently stretchy, as are a number of the decorative stitches. To straight stitch, use a longer stitch length and lower the tension settings. Use 100% polyester thread for the needle thread and woolly nylon in the bobbin. Straight stitches made using a double needle are also quite stretchy and give a nice finish to knits.

Use a fusible or double-stick seam tape to set knit seams. This will make handling easier and will minimize stretching during stitching.

HEMMING BULKY FABRICS

A single-fold hem (see Single-Fold Hem, page 29) is the best choice for bulky fabrics. To reduce bulk at the hem edge, hem tape or lace can be machine sewn to the raw edge of the fabric and then blindstitched to the garment (see Blindstitch Hem, page 20).

HEMMING GARMENTS

If you are working with a stretchy fabric or bias-cut design, it is best to let the garment hang overnight before marking the hem. Have the wearer try on the near-finished garment and mark the position of the bottom edge of the hem with one or more pins (if you are making the garment for yourself, enlist the help of another person). Determine the desired hem allowance and measure that amount down from the pin-marked finished length. Trim the fabric, making sure the cut is parallel to the floor.

HAND VS. MACHINE BLINDSTITCHING

Depending on the fabric, machine blindstitching may show through on the right side. To minimize the visibility of stitches, use matching thread and catch as little of the fabric as possible. For draperies and long, flowing gowns, the stitching may not be noticeable. For shorter, tailored skirts and dresses, hand stitching is the best way to get truly invisible results.

HEMMING CURVED EDGES

Curves can be difficult to fold into smooth hems. For narrow, curved hems use your fingers and your iron to manipulate the fabric prior to stitching. With convex (hill-shaped) curves, it is helpful to lightly gather the hem near the first fold line to ease the fold into place. Concave (valley-shaped) curves can sometimes be accommodated by gently stretching or lightly snipping the raw edge of the fabric. For wider curved hems, use bias tape (see Bias Tape, page 45) or create a facing that fits the curve exactly (see Adding Facings, page 103).

Fabric

Fiber Composition

Fabrics are made from either a single fiber type or a blend of two or more fibers. Natural fibers are derived from plants and animals, while synthetic fibers are polymers created by chemical processes. Fabrics made from 100% natural fibers are generally more comfortable and durable than their synthetic counterparts. Synthetic fabrics, however, are easier to care for and resist wrinkling. Blends often offer the best of both worlds.

Fiber Arrangement

WOVEN FABRIC

The fibers in woven fabrics are interlaced at right angles. Woven fabrics do not stretch except on the bias (diagonal direction). Crispness and weight are factors of the fiber size and of the tightness and pattern of weaving.

KNIT FABRIC

Fibers in knit fabrics are looped together. Knits have the ability to stretch, and they resist fraying when cut. The amount of stretch depends on the type of fiber and the looping pattern. Double-knit fabrics are quite stable, while single knits, such as interlock and jersey, are moderately stretchy. Rib knits and Lycra blends have a lot of stretch. Knits are primarily used for garment sewing.

FELT

Fibers in felt are matted together. Felt can be shaped or sewn, and it does not fray.

Fabric Fiber Composition

	FIBER TYPE	FEATURES	FABRIC TYPES
Natural	Cotton	Durable, soft, affordable, and comfortable to wear	Batiste, broadcloth, calico, canvas, corduroy, denim, flannel, gingham, interlock, jersey, muslin, poplin, sateen, seersucker, terry, velveteen, voile
	Silk	Fine sheen and luxurious drape	Charmeuse, chiffon, crepe de chine, dupioni, organza, shantung
	Linen	Strong, cool, and crisp with a distinct texture	Butcher's linen, damask, handkerchief linen, lawn, nubby linen
	Wool	Very warm and wrinkle resistant	Challis, crepe, felt, flannel, gabardine, tweed

	FIBER TYPE	FEATURES	FABRIC TYPES
Synthetic	Rayon	Soft and shiny, mimics natural fibers	Challis, jersey, numerous dress-weight fabrics, suitings, viscose
	Nylon	Strong and resilient, very versatile	Chiffon, lace, ripstop, sports fabrics, tulle, velvet
	Acetate	Very lustrous, drapes nicely	Faille, gauze, lining fabrics, taffeta, tricot, satin
	Polyester	Strong and wrinkle resistant, holds shape well	Charmeuse, chiffon, georgette, lining fabrics, organza, satin, single and double knits, taffeta
	Acrylic	Lightweight, soft, and warm	Felt, faux fur, fleece, indoor/outdoor canvas, suitings
	Spandex	Very elastic, generally used to add stretch to blends	Athletic fabrics, costume fabrics, stretch denim

Interfacing

Interfacings are classified as either fusible or sew-in. Fusible interfacings are ironed onto and become one with the fabric, making it easier to handle during the sewing process. It is important to choose a fusible interfacing that is compatible with the fabric and appropriate for the application—otherwise unsightly bubbles may appear on the right side of the item. Be sure to follow the manufacturer's instructions regarding iron temperature and pressing time.

Sew-in interfacings are basted into place and/or stacked so they are between layers of fabric in the finished garment. They are the best option for fine or heat-sensitive fabrics, or where softness is preferred over crispness. Thin fabrics such as organza and batiste may also be used as sew-in interfacing.

COMPANY KEY

C = C&T Publishing
F = Fashion Sewing Supply
H = HTC
P = Pellon

Interfacing Fiber Arrangement

Interfacings are categorized as nonwoven, woven, and knitted. Weft insertion interfacings are a combination of knitted loops in one direction and woven threads in the other.

INTERFACING TYPE	PROPERTIES
Nonwoven	Most affordable and easy to find. Can be cut in any direction and does not fray or stretch.
Woven	Adds crispness and allows for shaping. Available in stretch and nonstretch varieties.
Knit	Suitable for use with both knit and woven fabrics, moves and drapes nicely, resists bubbling, and holds up well to laundering.
Weft insertion	Drapes like a knit but has the stability of a woven. Can be textured for better adherence to textured fabrics.

Interfacing Weight

In apparel sewing, interfacing is lighter than the fashion fabric and is used to give body and/or stabilize specific parts of the garment, such as collars, cuffs, and facings. For accessories and home decor items, interfacing adds needed strength and weight, so it is often thicker than the face fabric. In fact, many of the heavyweight products are labeled as stabilizers rather than interfacings.

	WEIGHT	APPLICATIONS
Relative Weight	Very lightweight	Sheer garments; soft, drapey blouses and dresses; heirloom sewing; lingerie
	Lightweight	Light- to medium-weight blouses and dresses, fabrics that need just a bit of added body
	Mid-weight	Tailored shirts and jackets, handbag linings
	Heavyweight	Jackets and coats, handbags, belts
	Very heavyweight	Hat brims, boxes and bowls, fiber art

		FABRIC-WEIGHT PAIRING	FUSIBLE OR SEW-IN	PRODUCT NAME	COMPANY
INTERFACING	NONWOVEN	Sheer to light-weight fabrics	Fusible	Sheer D'Light Featherweight	H
				906F Fusible Sheerweight	P
			Sew-in	905 Sew-In Sheerweight	P
		Light to mid-weight fabrics	Fusible	Sheer D'Light Lightweight	H
				Fusi-Form Lightweight	H
				911FF Fusible Featherweight	P
				845F Designer's Lite	P
				880F Sof-Shape	P
				950F Shir-Tailor	P
			Sew-in	910 Sew-In Featherweight	P
				Intra-Face Light Weight	H
		Mid- to heavy-weight fabrics	Fusible	Sheer D'Light Medium Weight	H
				Fusi-Form Suitweight	H
				855F Tailor's Elite	P
				931TD Fusible Midweight	P
			Sew-in	930 Sew-In Midweight	P
				Intra-Face Medium Weight	H
		Crafts/accessories	Fusible	520 Deco-Fuse	P
				808 Craft-Fuse	P
				809 Décor-Bond	P
				71F Peltex I Ultra-Firm 1-Sided Fusible	P
				72F Peltex II Ultra-Firm 2-Sided Fusible	P
				Fuse-A-Shade	H
				Crafter's Choice	H
				fast2fuse (2 sided, 3 weights)	C
			Sew-in	Intra-Face Heavy Weight	H
				30, 40, 50, 65, & 70 Stabilizers	P
				70 Peltex Sew-In Ultra-Firm	P
				9260 Ultra-Firm	H
				Timtex	C
	WEFT	Light to mid-weight fabrics	Fusible	Whisper Weft	H
				Pro-Weft Supreme Light	F
		Mid- to heavy-weight fabrics	Fusible	860F Ultra Weft	P
				Pro-Weft Supreme Medium	F
				Armo Weft	H

INTERFACING

	FABRIC-WEIGHT PAIRING	FUSIBLE OR SEW-IN	PRODUCT NAME	COMPANY
KNIT	Sheer to light-weight fabrics	Fusible	Sheer-Knit	P
			So-Sheer	H
			Pro-Sheer Light	F
	Light to mid-weight fabrics	Fusible	Fusi-Knit	H
			Sof-Knit	H
			Easy-Knit	P
			Pro-Tricot Deluxe	F
WOVEN	Sheer to light-weight fabrics	Fusible	Pro-Sheer Elegance	F
			Touch O'Gold II	H
		Sew-in	Pro-Silk Organza	F
	Light to mid-weight fabrics	Fusible	Pro-Sheer Elegance Medium	F
			Bi-Stretch Lite	P
			Shape-Flex	C
			Pro-Woven Light-Crisp	F
		Sew-in	Veri-Shape	H
			SF785 Woven Sew-In	P
			Pro-Woven Superior Sew-In Lightly Soft	F
			Pro-Woven Superior Sew-In Lightly Crisp	F
	Mid- to heavy-weight fabrics	Fusible	Form-Flex All Purpose	H
			Acro Hair Canvas	H
			Pro-Tailor Classic Hair Cloth/Canvas Fusible	F
			HC120F Fusible Hair Canvas	P
		Sew-in	Tailor's Pride Hair Canvas	H
			HC110 Sew-In Hair Canvas	P
			Pro-Woven Superior Sew-In Medium	F
			Pro-Tailor Classic Sew-In Hair Cloth/Canvas	F

Other Fusible Products

Fusible webbing
Lightweight network of fibers, such as Wonder-Under (Pellon) and Stitch Witchery (Dritz), that adheres one layer of fabric to another.

Fusible adhesive
Similar to fusible webbing but in the form of a thin, solid sheet, such as HeatnBond (Thermoweb). Both are used for appliqué work and turn any fabric into a fusible interfacing. Fusibles can also be found in tape form for hemming and stabilizing seams.

Fusible fleece
Thick, soft batting-like material that can be adhered to fabric on one or both sides. Often used in handbag making and home decor, it provides structure similar to heavyweight interfacing but is soft and flexible. Products include 987F (Pellon), 9720-1 (HTC), Fusible Warm Fleece (Warm Company), and Insul-Fleece (C&T Publishing).

Fusible interfacing strips
Make It Simpler Fusible Interfacing (C&T Publishing) comes in a handy roll precut to 1½˝ × 15 yards.

Stuffing

Polyester Fiberfill
Poly fiberfill is the most widely available stuffing on the market. It is affordable and has a high loft, meaning it does not take much stuffing to fill a space. It can be difficult to stuff into small items such as dolls and plush toys because it does not pack well. For standard-sized pillows, prestuffed pillow forms are a good option (see Throw Pillows, page 77).

Natural-Fiber Stuffing
Stuffings made from 100% cotton or 100% wool tend to pack better and are ideal for dolls and stuffed animals.

Poly Pellets
Poly pellets add weight and can be used alone or as a base under fiber stuffing.

Batting

Batting Fiber Type

TYPE	ADVANTAGES	DISADVANTAGES
Polyester	Warm, holds up well to washing, easy to quilt, does not require extensive quilting for stability, inexpensive, available in many loft options	Does not breathe or drape like natural fibers, may be perceived as too hot, fibers tend to break down over time
Cotton, bamboo, cotton/ bamboo blend	Long lasting; supple drape; breathable yet warm and draft blocking; gives a flat, traditional look that shows off stitching detail. Cotton is relatively inexpensive. Bamboo is eco-friendly.	Can be difficult to quilt, not many loft options, does not rebound if flattened, requires closely spaced quilting to keep fibers in place, may shrink
Cotton/ synthetic blend	Combines the softness and breathability of cotton with the warmth, stability, and consistency of synthetics	Some shrinkage but not as much as 100% natural fiber battings
Wool	Very resilient (releases fold lines easily), breathable, long lasting, puffy texture	Tends to shrink, more expensive than cotton, may attract moths

Batting Thickness

THICKNESS	FEATURES
Low loft	Flat appearance that shows off stitching detail; good for wall hangings, table runners, place mats, and bed quilts; can also be used in quilted garments
Medium loft	Good for general-purpose quilting, including bed quilts; warmer than low-loft batting; easier to stitch than high-loft batting
High loft	Puffy, downlike appearance; can be difficult to stitch; often used for hand-tied quilts

Relative Loft

Fusible batting is fusible on one or both sides and eliminates or greatly reduces the need for basting. It prevents slippage and puckering during machine stitching.

Gathering

Marking Gathers

For accurate distribution of gathers, both the fabric to be gathered and the fabric to be attached should be divided into sections and marked.

Option 1	Option 2	Option 3
Notches are an efficient way to mark fabric, but they tend to get lost in the gathers in wide fabrics.	Straight pins may be placed perpendicular to the fabric edge at the marking point, but take care that they don't slip out during handling.	For fabrics that can withstand ironing and hold a crease, press marking can be used to make visible creases as reference points.

1. Fold the fabric in half widthwise.

2. Notch, pin, or press at the position of the fold. Open out the fabric. Bring the ends in to meet at the center and mark the resulting folds.

3. Unfold the strip. The 3 reference points divide the fabric into fourths.

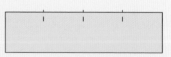

NOTE To divide into more sections, bring adjacent pins/ends together and mark the additional folds.

Straight-Stitch Gathering

1. Using a long stitch length and a loose tension setting, sew a row of gathering stitches near the edge. Sew a second row parallel to the first. Be sure to leave 2″–3″ tails at the beginning and end of each row.

TIPS
- Position the gathering stitches so that the seam will fall right between them. For example, for a ½″ seam allowance, place the gathering threads ¼″ and ¾″ from the edge.
- Use a contrasting thread color in the bobbin.

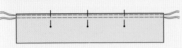

2. Grasp the bobbin threads and push the fabric toward the center on one side.

NOTE Do *not* pull the needle threads once you have pulled the bobbin threads, or the stitching will lock and/or break.

3. Grasp the bobbin thread on the other side and push the fabric toward the center.

4. The top edge of the gathered piece should be about the same length as the fabric to which it will be attached.

Zigzag-Stitch Gathering

1. Cut a piece of sturdy floss (embroidery or dental) longer than the edge. Pin at one end.

2. Using zigzag stitches (widest width and longest length settings), stitch near the edge of the fabric, with the floss centered beneath the presser foot. Stitch over the floss, not through it.

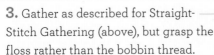

3. Gather as described for Straight-Stitch Gathering (above), but grasp the floss rather than the bobbin thread.

Attaching Gathers

1. Pull the threads to make the gathered fabric the same width as the piece that will be attached to it.

2. Place the pieces right sides together and align the appropriate edges. Match the ends and the marking points and pin the layers together.

3. Evenly distribute the gathers and use additional pins to secure.

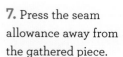

4. Stitch using the appropriate seam allowance and a normal stitch length and tension.

NOTE Avoid sewing over the basting stitches (straight-stitch method) or the floss (zigzag-stitch method).

5. After stitching, remove the pins and basting threads or floss.

6. Finish the raw edges with a zigzag or overlock stitch.

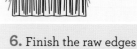

7. Press the seam allowance away from the gathered piece.

8. *Optional:* Set the seam allowance into place by topstitching along the seamline on the right side.

Ruffles

Hemmed Ruffles

Desired Finished Width + Hem Allowance + Seam Allowance
= Starting Width of Ruffle

 Hem the bottom edge of the ruffle prior to gathering. The most common hem finish is a thin double fold with straight stitching. Rolled hems are also a good option and can be covered with decorative thread using an overlock machine (see Rolled Hem, page 29).

Double-Thickness Ruffles

(Desired Finished Width + Seam Allowance) × 2
= Starting Width of Ruffle

 Fold the ruffle strip in half lengthwise, wrong sides together, prior to gathering. The raw edges are at the top, and the fold is at the bottom. This method is good for reversible projects and for sheer fabrics.

Bias-Cut Ruffles

Desired Finished Width + Seam Allowance
= Starting Width of Ruffle

 Cut the ruffle strip at 45° for a raw edge that does not fray and, therefore, does not require hemming. The resulting ruffle has a bit more body than one cut on the straight grain.

Ruffle Fullness

Ruffle fullness is described in terms of a "fullness factor."

Fullness Factor = Starting Strip Length ÷ Gathered Ruffle Length

For example, a 40˝ strip gathered to 20˝ has a fullness factor of 2, which is often expressed as 2x because the starting fabric is twice as long as the finished ruffle (b). As the fullness factor increases, the gathering becomes tighter and the ruffle becomes "fluffier." A ruffle with a fullness factor of 1.25x (a) is slightly gathered, while a ruffle with a fullness factor of 4x (c) is tightly gathered.

Thin fabrics can be gathered to a much higher fullness than thick fabrics. Similarly, single-thickness ruffles can be gathered to a higher fullness than double-thickness ruffles. The fullness factor you select depends on the fabric, the type of ruffle, and where it will be used.

Desired Gathered Length × Fullness Factor = Starting Strip Length

Bias Tape

Pre-folded bias tape can be purchased in a range of widths and colors. It is convenient and relatively affordable, but the feel is a bit stiff and the color choices are limited. Bias tape can be made from most fabrics, giving the sewist more control over its color and texture.

Single-fold bias tape has its long edges folded in toward the center. It usually does not show on the outside of the item.

Single-fold bias tape

Double-fold bias tape has its long edges folded in toward the center and then is folded again in half lengthwise. It is often used to encase raw edges. (See Folding Bias Tape, page 49.)

Double-fold bias tape

DESIRED FINISHED WIDTH	STARTING BIAS STRIP WIDTH	
	FOR SINGLE FOLD*	FOR DOUBLE FOLD**
¼″	⅝″	1⅛″
⅜″	⅞″	1⅝″
½″	1⅛″	2⅛″
¾″	1⅝″	3⅛″

* (Desired Finished Width × 2) + ⅛″
  = Starting Width for Single-Fold Tape

** (Desired Finished Width × 4) + ⅛″
   = Starting Width for Double-Fold Tape

NOTE When covering straight edges, you can use straight-grain tape (strips cut selvage to selvage) rather than bias tape. However, I prefer to use bias tape even on straight edges because I think it "hugs" the edge and moves better than straight-grain tape. In addition, the bias tape edges don't fray during the attachment process.

Cutting and Joining Bias Strips

METHOD 1

This method is quick and accurate for cutting shorter lengths. Use the table (at right) to determine the starting square size.

STARTING SQUARE	LENGTH OF STRIPS (1ST CUT)
9″ × 9″	12″
18″ × 18″	24¾″
27″ × 27″	37½″
36″ × 36″	50¼″
45″ × 45″	63″

1. Fold the square of fabric diagonally, right sides together.

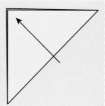

2. Make a second diagonal fold. Press.

3. Using a rotary cutter and clear ruler, trim ¼″ from the layers of fabric at the first folded edge.

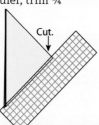

Cut.

4. Position the ruler so the edge is the desired tape width's distance from the first cut (see Cut Bias-Strip Width table, page 47) and make a second cut.

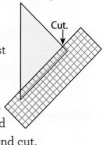

Cut.

5. This will yield 2 strips that are equal in length.

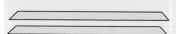

6. Continue cutting the folded square for more strips. Each set of strips will decrease in length.

7. Before joining the 2 strips, make sure the ends are cut at parallel 45° angles.

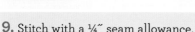

8. Place the strips right sides together and align the angled edges, leaving a ¼″ overhang on each side.

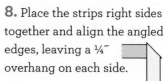

9. Stitch with a ¼″ seam allowance.

10. Press the seam allowance open.

11. Trim the seam allowance even with the sides of the strips.

METHOD 2

Use the table below to determine the starting square size needed to generate the desired continuous yardage for a given strip width.

FABRIC SQUARE SIZE	Cut Bias-Strip Width					
	1⅛″	1⅝″	2⅛″	2⅜″	3⅛″	4⅝″
	Total Length of Bias Strip Needed					
18″ × 18″	7⅛ yards	4⅞ yards	3½ yards	3⅜ yards	2½ yards	1⅜ yards
22″ × 22″	10¾ yards	7½ yards	5¾ yards	5 yards	3⅜ yards	2½ yards
26″ × 26″	15⅜ yards	10⅝ yards	8 yards	7 yards	5 yards	3 yards
30″ × 30″	20¾ yards	14⅜ yards	10½ yards	9⅜ yards	7 yards	4½ yards
34″ × 34″	26¾ yards	18½ yards	14⅛ yards	12⅝ yards	9⅛ yards	6½ yards
38″ × 38″	33¾ yards	23⅜ yards	17⅞ yards	16 yards	11⅞ yards	7⅜ yards
42″ × 42″	41½ yards	28⅝ yards	21⅜ yards	19⅝ yards	14¾ yards	9¾ yards

1. Cut the square in half diagonally.

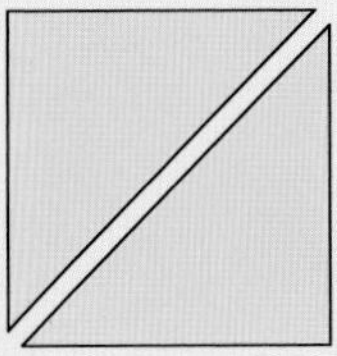

2. Place the triangles right sides together and align the original top and bottom edges.

3. Stitch a ¼″ seam.

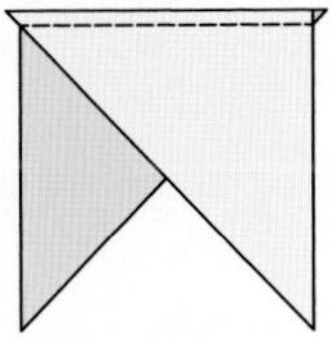

4. Press the seam allowance open.

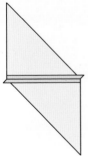

Method 2 steps continued on page 48.

5. Use a clear ruler and a marking tool to make lines on the wrong side of the fabric. Space the lines the desired tape width's distance apart, starting from the top edge.

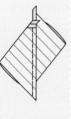

6. Fold the side edges back ¼˝ to the marked side and press.

7. With the marked sides facing out, butt the folded edges together. Shift so that the top edge meets the first line, the first line meets up with the second line, and so on.

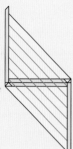

8. Carefully lift up the folds and pin at the creases. Stitch together with a ¼˝ seam along the crease.

9. Use scissors to cut along the marked lines to create a long continuous bias strip.

Folding Bias Tape

SINGLE-FOLD BIAS TAPE

Fold the long edges toward the center to achieve the desired finished width. A manual or automatic bias-tape maker is helpful for folding long lengths of tape.

Single-fold bias tape

DOUBLE-FOLD BIAS TAPE

1. Make single-fold tape that is twice the desired finished width.

2. Fold in half lengthwise, so that one side is slightly wider than the other.

Double-fold bias tape

Applying Bias Tape

APPLYING SINGLE-FOLD BIAS TAPE

1. Open out one fold in the tape. With right sides together, align the opened edge of the tape with the edge of the fabric to be finished. Pin into place.

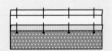

2. Stitch in the crease.

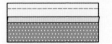

3. Fold the entire tape to the wrong side so that it does not show on the front. Press.

4. Edgestitch into place on the wrong side.

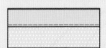

NOTE If you would like for the tape to end up on the right side of the finished item, start with the right side of the tape facing the wrong side of the fabric.

Applying Double-Fold Bias Tape

1. Open out the fold on the slightly narrower side of the tape.

2. With right sides together, align the opened edge of the tape with the edge of the fabric to be finished. Pin into place.

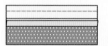

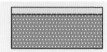

3. Stitch in the crease.

4. Fold the tape to the wrong side of the fabric. Half of the tape will show on the right side and half will show on the wrong side. Press.

5. Edgestitch into place on the right side. The stitching will catch the slightly longer edge on the back.

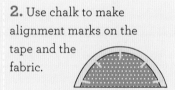

Navigating Curves with Bias Tape

It can be tricky to apply stretchy bias tape to concave and convex curves. Shaping and marking the bias tape first will help to make the application easier.

1. With right sides up, place the folded bias tape along the seamline of the curve. Press the tape to set the curve.

2. Use chalk to make alignment marks on the tape and the fabric.

3. Remove the tape and open out the chalk-marked fold. Extend markings to the edges of the tape and the fabric.

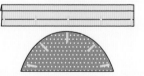

4. With right sides together, match the tape and fabric at the markings. Pin into place.

5. Stitch into place (see Applying Single-Fold Bias Tape, page 49, or Applying Double-Fold Bias Tape, above).

TURNING SQUARE CORNERS WITH BIAS TAPE

1. Begin stitching the bias tape into place on one of the sides (see Applying Single-Fold Bias Tape, page 49, or Applying Double-Fold Bias Tape, page 50). Leave a "tail" of unstitched bias tape at the beginning.

2. Continue stitching the bias tape toward the corner, but stop a seam-allowance distance from the corner and backstitch.

3. Fold the tape up to make a 45° fold at the corner and pin into place.

4. Fold the tape down to make a fold in line with the top edge. Align the edge of the tape with the edge of the fabric.

5. Stitch into place.

6. Complete the other 3 corners in the same way.

7. When you return to the edge where you began, leave several inches of space between the start and stop points. Leave another tail of bias tape at the end.

8. Join the ends (see Connecting Ends of Bias Tape, page 52).

9. Fold the bias tape to the wrong side. From the wrong side, fold the tape into place at the first edge, arranging the fold at the corner into a 45° angle.

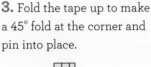

Wrong side

10. Fold the tape at the next edge, forming a 45° miter in the corner. Continue with the remaining sides.

Wrong side

11. Edgestitch into place.

1. Apply the bias tape, leaving several inches of space between the stitching start and stop points. Leave tails of bias tape at the beginning and end.

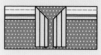

2. Trim the tails to parallel 45° angles that overlap by ½″ when the ends lie flat and in line with the edge of the fabric.

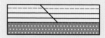

3. Lift the ends of the tape, right sides together, and join with a ¼″ seam. (See Cutting and Joining Bias Strips, Step 8, page 46.)

4. Finger-press the seam allowance open and trim the protruding points.

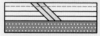

5. Fold and stitch into place.

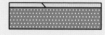

Piping

Piping is cording covered with bias strips. The bias strip width depends on the diameter of the cording and the desired seam allowance:

(Cording Diameter × 3) + (Desired Seam Allowance × 2)
= Starting Bias Strip Width

NOTES • It is helpful to convert fractions into decimals and then convert the result back to fractions (see Decimals to Fractions, page 123). For example, to make piping with ⅛″-diameter cording and a ¼″ seam allowance: (.125 × 3) + (.25 × 2) = .875 (⅞″)

• For small curved items, piping seam allowances should be kept small (less than ¼″) for more accurate placement.

• If the finished item will be washed, cotton cording should be preshrunk prior to covering.

Making Piping

1. Cut the bias strip or strips (see Cutting and Joining Bias Strips, pages 46 and 47).

2. Fold in half lengthwise, wrong sides together, and press.

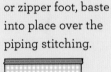

3. Insert the cording into the fold so it is snug against the crease. Use a piping foot or a zipper foot to stitch as close to the cording as possible.

Inserting Piping into a Straight Seam

1. Lay out the fabric right side up. Align the raw edge of the piping seam allowance with the raw edge of the fabric. Pin into place.

2. Using a piping or zipper foot, baste into place over the piping stitching.

3. Place the second piece of fabric on top of the first, right sides together. Use the piping or zipper foot to stitch the layers together over the existing stitching.

4. Open out the fabric and fluff the piping.

Inserting Piping around Corners

1. To apply piping to square or rectangular items such as pillow covers and place mats, first round off any square corners. Lay out the top piece right side up.

2. Align the raw edge of the piping seam allowance with the edge of the item. Allow for a bit more piping than needed to go around the corners. It will looked "squished" and wrinkled at this point but will stretch out and lie nicely in the finished item.

3. Leave tails at the start and stop points and overlap them in a crisscross fashion.

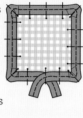

4. Stitch the piping into place, keeping the same seam allowance over the crossed ends.

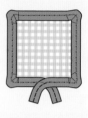

5. Place the other piece of fabric on top and stitch into place. Leave an opening on one side for turning.

6. Trim the crossed ends of the piping even with the seam allowance.

7. Turn right side out. Hand stitch the opening closed.

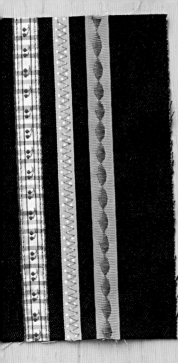

Trims

Flat Trims

Flat trims may be topstitched directly to a fabric or included in a seam. Examples include rickrack, lace, gimp, ribbon, and braiding.

SEWING TIPS FOR TRIMS

If possible, apply trims prior to assembly so that the ends are contained within seams.

Mark flat trim placement with a crease or a thin marker line prior to application.

Pin or hand baste the trim into place along the marking. Depending on the weight of the trim, glue or double-stick basting tape may be used instead.

Don't limit yourself to straight stitches for attaching trim. Zigzags are often easier to stitch and give a better hold, especially with thin trims. Decorative stitches can be used as well. Multiple rows of stitching may be required for wide trims.

Edgings

Edgings have a decorative edge and a utilitarian binding or allowance for attachment. They are designed to be included in a seam or positioned behind a hem but can be topstitched into place on the right side of an item if the binding edge is attractive. Examples of edgings include gathered lace and eyelet, corded edging, and pearl edging.

SEWING TIPS FOR EDGINGS

NOTE When you are trimming square or rectangular items, thin edgings can be treated like piping (see Inserting Piping around Corners, page 54). For wider ruffled edgings, be sure to bunch the trim at the corners so that it will fan out properly in the finished item.

1. To insert an edging into a seam, position the inside edge of the edging allowance on the seamline of the item before assembly. Pin the trim into place, leaving an overlap at the ends.

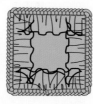

2. Stitch into place, starting and stopping about 1˝ on each side of the end meeting point. Trim so that the ends overlap by ½˝.

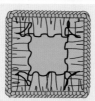

3. Place the ends right sides together and stitch with a ¼˝ seam allowance.

4. Stitch the unsewn trim into place.

5. Place the other piece of fabric on top and finish (see Inserting Piping around Corners, Steps 5–7, page 54).

Fringes

Fringes have dangling elements attached to a woven strip. They can be placed behind a trim or topstitched into place. Examples include ball, brush, and beaded fringes.

SEWING TIPS FOR FRINGES

Trim the fringe at the ends, as needed, to work into seams. For shorter fringes, a zipper foot may be needed for installation.

Insertions

Insertions are designed to join two pieces of fabric and are often used in heirloom sewing. Usually lace or eyelet, they can be connected by seams or zigzag topstitching.

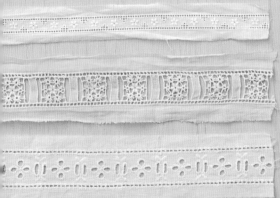

SEWING TIPS FOR INSERTIONS

As with any lace or eyelet, insertions have a right (prettier) and wrong (more knotty) side.

Zippers

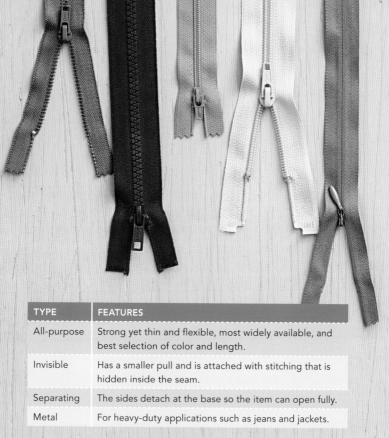

TYPE	FEATURES
All-purpose	Strong yet thin and flexible, most widely available, and best selection of color and length.
Invisible	Has a smaller pull and is attached with stitching that is hidden inside the seam.
Separating	The sides detach at the base so the item can open fully.
Metal	For heavy-duty applications such as jeans and jackets.

Zipper Length

If you are working with a separating zipper, purchase the exact length needed or tailor your project to fit a standard zipper size. For other types of zippers, if the exact zipper length is not available, purchase a zipper that is a bit longer than you need. To shorten it, before inserting the zipper add a simple bar tack over the zipper teeth where you want the zipper to stop. Then trim the zipper below the bar tack.

Essential Sewing Reference Tool

Stitching Zippers

Zippers usually include an extra ⅝˝ of tape above the top stop for finishing with a ⅝˝ seam allowance. If the seam allowance is narrower, you can trim the tape. If the zipper is applied to an item with a finished top edge, simply fold the excess zipper tape over to the wrong side prior to stitching.

The zipper foot allows for stitching as close as possible to the zipper teeth without interfering with the zipper movement. Since the foot is relatively narrow, stitching can be difficult to control, especially if the needle is set to stitch far away from the foot. For best results, premark the stitching position with either a washable marker or hand basting stitches. For best control, configure the foot and needle so that they will clear the zipper parts but keep the stitching as close to the foot as possible. For couture garments, hand stitching may be substituted to give a nearly invisible finish.

NOTES If the fabric will not hold a crease, use basting tape, hand stitching, or glue to hold the seam allowance folds in place.

When snipping seam allowances, be careful to keep the snips within the actual seam allowance.

Centered Zipper Installation

1. Fold back the ⅝″ seam allowances on both edges of the fabric opening and press to set.

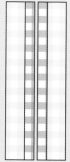

2. Butt the folds together, with the top edges aligned. Place the closed zipper on top of the folds, positioning the top edge of the zipper at the top edge of the fabric (or at the desired position).

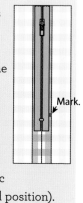

Mark.

3. Using a removable marker, mark one of the folded seam allowances, about ¼″ above the bottom zipper stop (see Step 2). Extend the mark across to the edge of the other seam allowance and then snip the seam allowances at the marks.

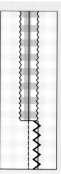

Snip. Snip.

4. Align the edges below the markings and stitch together with a ⅝″ seam allowance. Edge finish as desired.

5. *Optional:* If the seam allowance is at least ½″, lightly trim the zipper seam allowances with pinking shears.

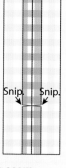

6. On the right side of the item, make a ½″ mark centered on the seam, just above the stitching.

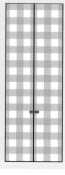

7. Extend the ends of the mark to the top edge, ¼˝ from the folds.

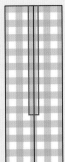

8. Unzip the zipper and apply glue to the length of the right-hand tape.

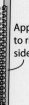

Apply glue to right-hand side.

9. With the right side of the item facing up, stick the right-hand fabric fold to the right-hand zipper tape. The fold should be in line with the teeth. Topstitch into place along the marking using a zipper foot.

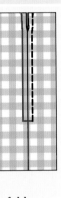

10. Apply glue to the left-hand side of the zipper tape. Close the zipper. Arrange the fabric folds so that they butt up against each other and align at the top. Stick the left-hand fabric fold to the zipper.

11. Starting at the bottom of the first line of stitching, top-stitch the zipper into place along the remaining marking.

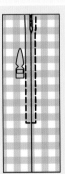

12. Stop stitching near the zipper stop at the top, leaving the needle in place. Lift the presser foot and open the zipper.

13. Lower the presser foot and complete the stitching.

Lapped Zipper Installation

1. Make a ½˝ fold in the left-hand side of the zipper opening. Press to set. Make a ¾˝ fold in the right-hand edge and press to set.

2. Butt the folds together, with the top edges aligned. Place the closed zipper on top of the folds, positioning the top edge of the zipper at the top of the fabric (or at the desired position).

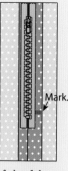

Mark.

3. Make a mark in one of the folded seam allowances, about ¼˝ above the bottom zipper stop (see Step 2). Extend the mark across to the edge of the other seam allowance and then snip the seam allowances at the marks.

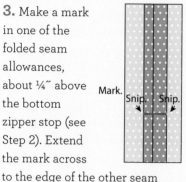

Mark. Snip. Snip.

4. Trim ¼˝ off the wider seam allowance (right-hand side) beneath the mark, so that it is ½˝ wide.

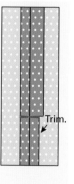

Trim.

5. Align the edges below the markings and stitch together with a ½˝ seam allowance. Edge finish as desired.

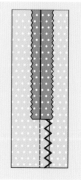

6. Open the zipper and apply glue to the length of the right-hand tape.

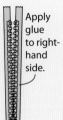

Apply glue to right-hand side.

7. With the right side of the fabric facing up, stick the right-hand fabric fold (the narrower fold) to the right-hand tape. The fold should be positioned about $1/16$″ from the teeth. Edgestitch into place using a zipper foot.

8. On the right side of the fabric, mark a line $1/2$″ from the left-hand fold, extending from the top edge of the zipper to the bottom of the opening. Draw a short line to connect this line to the edge of the fold just above the stitching.

9. Zip the zipper and arrange the fold so it just overlaps the stitching on the other side. Pin into place.

10. Carefully topstitch into place along the marking.

Invisible Zipper Installation

1. Finish the edges of the zipper opening as desired. Mark the seamline below the zipper opening on the wrong side of each piece.

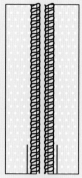

2. Open the zipper and place it flat with the pull side facing up. Apply glue to the length of the right-hand tape.

Apply glue.

3. With the pull side facing the right side of the fabric, align the outer edge of the right-hand tape with the finished edge of the right-hand side of the fabric opening.

4. Note that there is a small fold near the teeth; use an iron to press it open.

5. Using a zipper foot (either standard or invisible), stitch very close to the teeth.

6. Stop stitching when the foot nears the pull.

7. Turn the zipper over so the pull is facing up. Fold open the fabric attached to the right hand side. Do not press. Apply glue to the length of the left-hand tape.

Apply glue to left-hand side.

8. Turn the zipper over and place it on the remaining fabric piece, right sides together. Align the outer edge of the tape with the finished edge of the left-hand side of the fabric opening. Press the zipper and stitch (see Steps 4–6, page 64).

9. Turn the zipper and fabric to the right side, and pull the fabric away from the teeth. Close the zipper.

10. With the end of the zipper pulled out of the way, align the fabric below the zipper stitching.

11. Stitch on the marked seam allowance from the bottom edge to just beyond the zipper stitching.

Buttonholes and Buttons

Buttonholes

Sizing Buttonholes

For standard flat buttons, buttonholes should be about ¼″ larger than the button diameter. For thick or odd-shaped buttons, the buttonholes may need to be a bit larger. It is always best to make test buttonholes on scrap fabric first.

Buttonhole Placement

If you are working with a pattern, the button size and placement will be specified. For modifications or your own designs, here are a few guidelines to keep in mind.

Vertical buttonholes are used mostly on shirt plackets where there is not enough room for a horizontal buttonhole. Use horizontal buttonholes on most garments, particularly on those that are fitted or closely fitted.

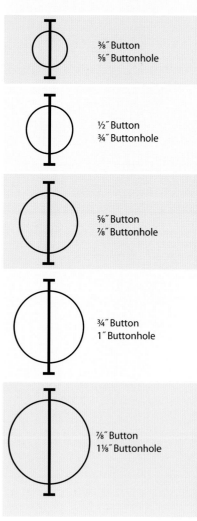

This diagram is actual size and can be used as a gauge for measuring buttons or as a template for tracing buttonholes.

⅜″ Button
⅝″ Buttonhole

½″ Button
¾″ Buttonhole

⅝″ Button
⅞″ Buttonhole

¾″ Button
1″ Buttonhole

⅞″ Button
1⅛″ Buttonhole

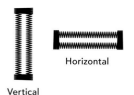

Horizontal

Vertical

BUTTONHOLE SPACING

If you are unsure of how many buttons to use, take a look at similar garments in your wardrobe.

1. Choose the number of buttons you want to use. Subtract 1 from this number to determine how many between-button spaces you will have.

2. Measure the placket from the top button position to the bottom button position.

3. Divide this measurement by the number of *spaces* to determine the length of the spaces.

BUTTONHOLE LOCATION

Buttons and buttonholes usually meet right at the centerline, unless the garment has an intentionally offset placket. For men's garments, the buttonholes are on the right-hand placket; for women's garments, they are on the left-hand placket, as shown.

Men's   Women's

Marking Buttonholes

1. If you are not using a premarked pattern, make a paper template that has properly spaced line drawings of the buttonholes.

2. Use a thick needle to pierce the pattern or template at the ends and centers of the buttonholes.

3. Align the pattern or template with the right side of the fabric and use a fine washable marker or chalk pencil to mark the fabric through the holes. Connect the dots.

4. Another option is to fold the pattern or template at the buttonhole line, place it on the garment next to the proper position, and mark just beside the fold.

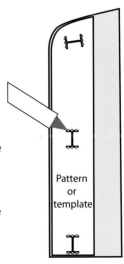

Pattern or template

Stitching Buttonholes

The typical buttonhole is made of two rows of zigzag stitches flanked by bar tacks (wider and tighter zigzag stitches). The buttonhole slit is made after stitching.

Buttonholes can be made manually on a sewing machine by sewing zigzag stitches at the desired size and width settings. Most machines, however, come with preprogrammed buttonhole-making capabilities.

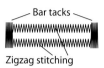

FOUR-STEP BUTTONHOLES

Usually found on basic mechanical sewing machines, the needle position and stitch width are preset for each step of the buttonholing process. The user determines the stitching length and duration.

1. Sew a bar tack.

2. Zigzag stitch to form one side of the buttonhole.

3. Sew the second bar tack.

4. Zigzag stitch to form the other side of the buttonhole.

ONE-STEP BUTTONHOLES

The change in stitch width and needle position occurs automatically when a part of the buttonhole foot bumps into a sensor on the machine. Buttonhole sizing is dependent on manual settings or the diameter of the button, which may be held in the foot during stitching. One disadvantage of the button-size method is that it does not take button thickness into consideration, so a larger button might have to be used as a stand-in to get a big enough buttonhole.

TIPS

- Always place interfacing behind fabric before stitching buttonholes to prevent puckering and distortion of stitches. In most plackets and cuffs, interfacing is already sandwiched between the layers of fabric.

- Use matching thread to minimize the appearance of imperfections.

- Do not stretch or pull fabric during the buttonholing process. If the fabric seems to be "sticking," use a layer of tear-away stabilizer under the item you are buttonholing.

- After making the buttonholes, remove the markings following the manufacturer's directions. Apply a touch of Fray Check to set the stitching. After it dries, use a pair of small sharp scissors to make the slit.

- A seam ripper may be used to make the slit, but be careful not to cut the bar tacks. Pins may be placed through the bar tacks for extra protection.

Buttons

> **TIP: Thread**
> For a strong, secure attachment, sew on buttons with thick thread made specifically for buttons and crafts.

Attaching Flat Buttons

Flat buttons have two or four holes and are usually about ⅛˝ thick.

1. Mark the desired position of the button on the wrong side of the item.

2. Insert about 24˝ of thread into a hand sewing needle. Match the ends and tie into 1 or 2 knots. Insert the needle from the back of the fabric at the marking and pull the thread through to the knot.

3. Run the needle up through one hole and down through another, then back into the fabric.

> **NOTE** For four-hole buttons, make stitches through holes that are across from one another diagonally, not side by side.

4. Insert a toothpick through the stitch, between the button and the fabric. Bring the needle back through the fabric and make a stitch through the other pair of holes (4-hole button) or the previous pair (2-hole button). Repeat the stitching process once more for each set of holes.

Toothpick

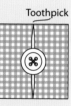

5. Tie 1 or 2 knots on the wrong side of the item.

6. Remove the toothpick. Bring the needle through the fabric and wind it around the stitches under the button to form a shank.

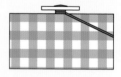

7. Reinsert the needle into the fabric and tie 1 or 2 knots on the back.

> **TIP: Attaching Buttons by Machine**
> Flat buttons can also be sewn into place by machine using the appropriate foot, dropped feed dogs, and a tight zigzag stitch. Consult your sewing machine's owner's manual for specific information.

Attaching Shank Buttons

Shank buttons have a raised channel or loop on the back of the button.

1. See Steps 1 and 2 in Attaching Flat Buttons (page 70).

2. Run the needle through the shank and then back down through the fabric. Repeat the stitching process 2 or 3 more times.

3. Tie 1 or 2 knots on the back side of the item.

Bed Coverings

Bed and Bedding Sizes

BED SIZE	MATTRESS	COMFORTER	COVERLET	BEDSPREAD
	SIZE MEASUREMENTS LISTED IN INCHES			
Youth (toddler)	32 × 66	56 × 78	64 × 92	74 × 97
Studio/cot	30 × 75	54 × 87	62 × 101	72 × 106
Bunk	38 × 75	62 × 87	70 × 101	80 × 106
Twin	39 × 75	63 × 87	71 × 101	81 × 106
Twin, X-long	39 × 80	63 × 92	71 × 106	81 × 111
Twin, wide	48 × 75	72 × 87	80 × 101	90 × 106
Double (full)	54 × 75	78 × 87	86 × 101	96 × 106
Double, X-long	54 × 80	78 × 92	86 × 106	96 × 111
Queen	60 × 80	84 × 92	92 × 106	102 × 111
King	78 × 80	102 × 92	110 × 106	120 × 111
California king	72 × 84	96 × 96	104 × 110	114 × 115

Comforters cover the mattress but not the box spring. Coverlets cover the mattress and the box spring, and have additional length so that the pillow can be covered and a tuck made beneath it. Bedspreads are like coverlets but extend almost to the floor. Duvets cover a premade comforter.

Yardage Requirements

The chart below gives the total yardage needed for each type of bedding. Divide the yardage into the number of equal lengths shown in parentheses. Additional yardage may be needed to match large prints. For double-sided bedding, purchase a like amount of fabric for the backing.

Piece the lengths together vertically to achieve the needed minimum width. Determine the exact desired finished width and length based on the Bed and Bedding Sizes chart (page 72) and personal preference.

BED SIZE	FABRIC WIDTH		
	43″–45″	54″–60″	104″–110″
Twin			
Comforter or duvet	5 yards (2)	5 yards (2)	2⅝ yards (1)
Coverlet or bedspread	6 yards (2)	6 yards (2)	3⅛ yards (1)
Full			
Comforter or duvet	5 yards (2)	5 yards (2)	2⅝ yards (1)
Coverlet or bedspread	9 yards (3)	6 yards (2)	3⅛ yards (1)
Queen			
Comforter or duvet	5¼ yards (2)	5¼ yards (2)	2¾ yards (1)
Coverlet or bedspread	9⅜ yards (3)	6⅜ yards (2)	3¼ yards (1)
King			
Comforter or duvet	7⅞ yards (3)	5¼ yards (2)	2¾ yards (1)
Coverlet or bedspread	9⅜ yards (3)	9⅜ yards (3)	6⅜ yards (2)

Example:

A twin-size comforter or duvet will require 5 yards of 44″-wide fabric for the top. Cut this fabric into 2 pieces, each 2½ yards. Remove the selvages then join the 2 pieces along their long sides using a ½″ seam allowance. The result will be a large piece measuring 87″ × 2½ yards. Trim to desired size.

Basic Comforter

1. Add 1˝ to the desired finished length as well as the width to provide for seam allowances.

2. Cut 2 pieces of fabric (prejoined) and 1 piece of batting this size.

3. Place the 2 pieces of fabric right sides together, with the batting on top.

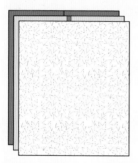

4. Stitch all the way around with a ½˝ seam allowance, leaving a 3˝ opening on one side. Trim the seam allowance near the corners.

5. Turn right side out, with the batting between the fabric layers.

6. Hand stitch the opening closed. Stitch or tie at regular intervals to secure the batting.

Hand stitch.

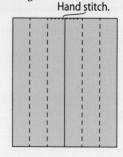

Hemmed Coverlet or Bedspread

1. Determine the desired hem allowance. Multiply by 2 and add to the desired finished dimensions.

2. Use the calculated dimensions to trim the prejoined fabric. If a lining is included, stack the lining and face fabric wrong sides together and baste around the edges.

3. Hem all 4 edges (see Hems, page 29) or bind with double-fold bias tape. (See Applying Double-Fold Bias Tape, page 50, and Turning Square Corners with Bias Tape, page 51.)

Quilted Coverlet or Bedspread

OPTION 1

Cut and construct a basic comforter (see Basic Comforter, page 74). Quilt as desired.

OPTION 2

1. Cut the prejoined fabric and batting a bit larger than the desired finished size.

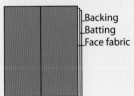

Backing
Batting
Face fabric

2. Sandwich the batting between the layers of fabric, wrong sides of fabric facing the batting. Quilt.

3. Trim to the desired finished size and finish with double-fold bias tape. (See Applying Double-Fold Bias Tape, page 50, and Turning Square Corners with Bias Tape, page 51.)

Basic Duvet

1. Add 2˝–4˝ to the length and width of the comforter. Add an additional double-fold hem allowance for the top edge.

2. Using the calculated dimensions, cut 2 pieces of prejoined fabric.

3. Place the 2 pieces of fabric right sides together. Stitch around the edge with a ½˝ seam allowance, leaving the top edge open.

4. Trim the seam allowance at the corners.

5. Hem each raw edge of the top opening individually. and add snaps, or buttonholes and buttons.

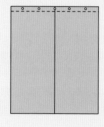

NOTE A zipper closure is also an option, but the zipper should be added before stitching the sides.

Pillows

Bed Pillow and Pillowcase Sizes

PILLOW	PILLOW SIZE	PILLOWCASE SIZE
	SIZE MEASUREMENTS LISTED IN INCHES	
Standard	20 × 26	21 × 32
Queen	20 × 30	21 × 36
King	20 × 36	21 × 42
California king	20 × 40	21 × 46

A pillowcase slips over the pillow with a fairly loose fit and has a side opening with an overhang. A sham is more fitted (it is the same size as the pillow) and often has a decorative ruffle or flange and a back opening (see Pillow Closure Options, page 79).

Making Basic Standard- and Queen-Size Pillowcases

1. Cut 2 pieces of fabric 22˝ × 38½˝ (standard size) or 22˝ × 42½˝ (queen size).

2. Place right sides together and stitch 1 short side and 2 long sides with a ½˝ seam allowance. Edge finish as desired.

3. Make a 3˝ double-fold hem on the open side. (See Double-Fold Hem, page 29.)

Throw Pillows

Prestuffed pillow forms make pillow-making easier and are available in a range of sizes and materials. For a tightly stuffed throw pillow, make a pillow cover that is an inch smaller than the form in each dimension when finished. For a softer pillow, make the finished cover the same size or slightly larger than the pillow form.

Pillows can also be made by first sewing a muslin cover and then filling it with stuffing (see Stuffing, page 38). For firm pillows, pack the stuffing tightly and evenly. For softer pillows, use less stuffing and fluff it while adding.

> **TIP**
> To give stuffed pillows a flatter, more even appearance, set the iron to a temperature that is appropriate for the outer fabric but hot enough to make steam. Press the pillow in sections.

Pillow Types

Basic pillow
Made from two square, rectangular, or rounded-corner pieces of fabric. Trims such as piping, edging, or ruffles can be added to the seams (see Edge Treatments, pages 40–57).

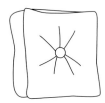

Box pillow
Has side panels that connect the top and bottom pieces and often includes decorative piping.

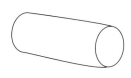

Bolster
Cylindrical pillow often used for neck support. It can be made from a rect-angle (joined at the long edge) that is attached to two circles at the ends, or from a single rectangular piece that is tied at the ends Tootsie Roll style.

Self-flanged pillow
Made as a basic pillow and then turned and stitched again a distance from the seam to create a flap (flange) around the entire pillow.

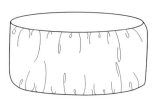

Pouf
Large cylindrical or cube-like pillow used as a chair or ottoman.

Tufted pillow
Has decorative buttons or tacking that forms dimples in the fabric.

Pillow Closure Options

Nonremovable pillow covers can be made by leaving an opening in the stitching during the construction process. Turn the cover right side out, insert the pillow form, and then neatly hand or machine stitch the opening closed.

Removable pillow covers can be made using one of the following techniques.

CENTER-LAPPED OPENING

1. Add ½˝ to the desired finished width and length. Cut the front piece to this size.

2. Using the same measurements, divide the length in half and add the overlap and a ½˝ hem allowance. For throw pillows the overlap is 3˝, for bed pillows, 4˝. Cut 2 pieces to this length and the original width.

3. Sew a ¼˝ double-fold hem on a short side of each of the large rectangles.

4. Place a hemmed piece on top of the front, right sides together. Align the raw edges and pin into place.

Pillow Back 1 (right side down)	Pillow Front (right side up)

5. Place the second hemmed piece on top of the first and align the raw edges with those of the pillow front. The 2 hemmed pieces will overlap to form the back opening.

Pillow Back 2

(right side down)

←→ overlap

6. Stitch around the outer edges with a ¼˝ seam allowance. Turn right side out.

End-Lapped Opening

1. Add ½″ to the desired finished width and length. Cut the front piece and 1 back piece to this size. Cut a second back piece that is the same width (short dimension) as the first but is only 4″ in length.

2. Sew a ¼″ double-fold hem on 1 side of each of the back pieces.

3. Place the large back piece on top of the front piece, right sides together. Align the raw edges and pin into place.

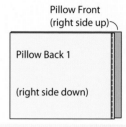

Pillow Front
(right side up)

Pillow Back 1

(right side down)

4. Place the small back piece on top of the first and align the raw edges with those of the pillow front.

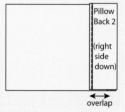

Pillow Back 2

(right side down)

overlap

5. Stitch around the outer edges with a ¼″ seam allowance. Turn right side out.

Lapped Opening with Buttons

1. Add ½″ to the desired finished length and width. Cut the front piece to this size.

2. Using the same measurements, divide the length in half and add the overlap and double-fold hem allowance. For throw pillows, add 3″ for the overlap and 3″ for the hem; for bed pillows, add 4″ for the overlap and 4″ for the hem. Cut 2 back pieces to this length and the original width.

3. Cut a strip of interfacing the width of the hem allowance (1½˝ for a small pillow, 2˝ for a large pillow). Sew or fuse interfacing to a short edge of Back 1 to stabilize the buttonhole area.

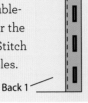

Back 1

4. Sew a double-fold hem over the interfacing. Stitch the buttonholes.

Back 1

5. Sew a double-fold hem in Back 2.

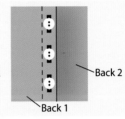

6. Assemble the pillow front and pillow back pieces. (See Center-Lapped Opening, page 79.)

Back 2

Back 1

7. Sew buttons to the Back 2 piece.

SIDE-ZIPPER OPENING

1. Add 1˝ to the desired finished length and width. Cut the front and back pieces to this size.

2. Select an invisible zipper that is 2˝–3˝ shorter than the finished width.

3. Attach the zipper in the center of a side seam. (See Invisible Zipper Installation, page 64.)

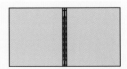

4. Open the zipper and stitch the remaining edges together with a ½˝ seam allowance.

5. Turn right side out through the zipper opening.

Bed Skirts

Bed skirts are composed of a top covering that sits between the mattress and box spring, and a drop (either a ruffle or straight piece of fabric) that extends from the top of the box spring to the floor on the sides and foot of the bed. Ruffled bed skirts have a continuous ruffle that is joined to the sides and foot of the bed skirt. Pleated bed skirts have pleats at the corners and one or more pleats at the foot and sides.

Purchased bed skirts have a drop length that ranges from 14˝ to 20˝. To determine the ideal drop length for your bed, measure from the top of the box spring to the floor. Add the seam and hem allowances to calculate the needed starting fabric strip width.

To calculate the finished (fully gathered or pleated) length of the bed skirt, multiply the side mattress dimension times 2, and add the foot mattress dimension. Multiply the finished length by the desired fullness (see Ruffle Fullness, page 44) to determine the starting length of the ruffle or pleat strip. Piece fabric to achieve the needed length.

The starting top covering fabric is cut the same size as the top of the box spring.

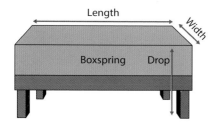

Curtains

Curtain Types

Curtains (also called drapes)
Lined or unlined panels of fabric that hang in front of a window.

Cafe curtains
Lined or unlined panels of fabric that cover only the bottom portion of a window.

Shower curtain
Unlined fabric or vinyl panel that covers a shower stall or tub enclosure.

Valance
Short, decorative fabric element that hangs above a window or curtain. Examples include balloon valances and swags.

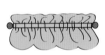
Balloon valance

Swag

Curtain Length Measurements and Hem Calculations

Curtains can hang from rod to floor (A), rod to baseboard (B), rod to sill (C), or rod to anywhere in between the sill and floor.

1. To determine the needed fabric length, measure from the top of the rod to the desired position of the bottom of the hem.

2. Add in the top seam, hem, or pocket allowance and the bottom hem allowance. If you are attaching the curtains with hardware such as hooks, tabs, or clips, subtract the length of the hardware.

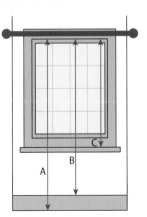

Curtain Width Measurements and Fullness Calculations

1. Measure from one end of the rod to the other. Do not include decorative elements such as finials.

2. Determine the desired fullness based on the type of fabric to be used and the look you want. Then calculate the ungathered width (see Ruffle Fullness, page 44).

> **Rod Length × Fullness Factor = Ungathered Width**

For most fabrics, a curtain that is twice the width of the rod (twice the fullness) will give ideal fullness. For thin, sheer fabrics, three times the fullness will give more privacy, and for thick fabrics, one and a half times the fullness might be adequate. For curtains that split in the middle, use half the width of the rod for fullness calculations for each side.

Curtain Hanging Options

Rod pocket
A pocket to accommodate the rod, created by folding over the top edge of the fabric like a hem that is open at the sides (see Hems, page 29).

Hanging sleeve
A strip of fabric sewn to the back of the curtain for rod insertion (similar to a rod pocket).

Buttonholes
Sewn into the curtain for use with rings or ties that attach to the rod.

Grommets
Metal rings inserted into the curtain to create holes for the rod to weave in and out of.

Tab tops
Looped strips sewn to the curtain (see Basic Tab-Top Curtains, page 85) for rod insertion.

Clips
Clothespin-like metal hardware attached to the top edge of the curtain. The hardware includes a ring at the top that hangs from the rod.

Basic Tab-Top Curtains

1. Determine the desired finished dimensions, keeping in mind that the top edge of the panel will fall 3″ below the rod. Add the allowances for side and bottom hems. Allow for a 1″ double-fold hem at the top (2″ hem allowance).

2. Cut the fabric and hem all sides.

3. Determine how many 1½″ tabs will be needed for 5″ maximum spacing (on center) using the following calculations:

Finished Panel Width ÷ (Maximum Spacing + 1)
= Number of Spaces (round to the nearest whole number)

Number of Spaces + 1 = Number of Tabs

Number of Tabs × Tab Width = Total Tab Width

Finished Panel Width - Total Tab Width = Total Space Width

Total Space Width ÷ Number of Spaces = Space Width

For example, dividing 43″ by 6 (maximum spacing + 1) gives 7.16, which rounds down to 7 spaces. Adding 1 to 7 gives 8 tabs. Multiplying 8 × 1½″ = 12″ (the total width of all the tabs placed side by side). Subtracting this number from 43″ (the panel width) gives 31″ (total space width). Dividing this number by 7 (the number of spaces) gives spacing of 4.4″.

Basic Tab-Tob Curtains steps continued on page 86.

4. For each tab, cut an 8½˝ × 3½˝ strip of fabric.

5. Fold in half lengthwise, right sides together. Stitch a ¼˝ seam on the long raw edges.

6. Turn right side out and press.

7. *Optional:* Topstitch ¼˝ from the long edges.

8. Bring the short ends together and join with zigzag stitches.

9. Place the tabs on the back side of the panel, with the zigzagged edge in line with the bottom of the top hem. Position the tabs using the spacing calculated in Step 3. Pin or gluestick each tab into place.

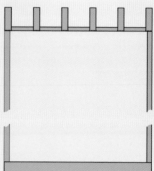

10. Stitching on the right side, stitch each tab into place using the following pattern:

1. Stitch a rectangle.

2. Stitch from one corner to another diagonally.

3. Stitch over the original stitching to the next corner.

4. Stitch from that corner diagonally to the remaining corner.

5. Stitch back to the start point.

Table Linens

Square or Rectangular Tablecloths

Unless the table is small and the fabric is wide, piecing is required to make a tablecloth. Generally, a center panel is flanked by two smaller side panels.

| Side panel |
| Center panel |
| Side panel |

TABLE SIZE RANGE	STANDARD TABLECLOTH SIZE	PIECE (# TO CUT): SIZE*	YARDAGE REQUIREMENTS**
25″ × 25″ to 40″ × 40″	52″ × 52″	Center (1): 43″ × 54″ Sides (2): 6″ × 54″ OR single piece 54″+ wide	3⅛ yards 1⅝ yards
28″ × 46″ to 40″ × 54″	52″ × 70″	Center (1): 43″ × 72″ Sides (2): 6″ × 72″ OR single piece 54″+ wide	4⅛ yards 2⅛ yards
36″ × 60″ to 48″ × 72″	70″ × 84″	Center (1): 43″ × 86″ Sides (2): 15″ × 86″	5 yards
36″ × 74″ to 48″ × 90″	70″ × 102″	Center (1): 43″ × 104″ Sides (2): 15″ × 104″	6 yards
36″ × 94″ to 48″ × 104″	70″ × 120″	Center (1): 43″ × 122″ Sides (2): 15″ × 122″	7 yards
36″ × 118″ to 48″ × 130″	70″ × 144″	Center (1): 43″ × 146″ Sides (2): 15″ × 146″	8¼ yards

* Includes ¼″ seam allowances and 1″ total hem allowance.

** 44″–54″+ widths, unless otherwise noted in "single piece" size in previous column.

More fabric may be required to match large prints.

Custom Tablecloth Sizing

Measure the length and width of the tabletop. Determine the desired drop (the length of fabric that hangs off the table top at the sides).

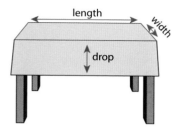

Determine the Finished Dimensions

Table Width + (Desired Drop × 2) = Desired Finished Width

Table Length + (Desired Drop × 2) = Desired Finished Length

Add the hem allowances to determine the cut dimensions:

Desired Finished Width + (Hem Allowance × 2) = Unhemmed Fabric Width

Desired Finished Length + (Hem Allowance × 2)
= Unhemmed Fabric Length

Panel Sizing and Assembly

The size of the center panel is a matter of personal preference and fabric width. If the width of the center panel is narrower than the width of the table, the seams will be positioned on the tabletop. Otherwise, the seams will be in the drop.

Determine the center panel width (cut size):

Desired Center Panel Width + (Seam Allowance × 2)
= Unhemmed Center Panel Width

Determine the side panel width (cut size):

[(Unhemmed Fabric Width - Center Panel Width) ÷ 2] + Seam Allowance
= Unhemmed Side Panel Width

1. Cut 1 piece the unhemmed center panel width × the unhemmed fabric length.

2. Cut 2 pieces the unhemmed side panel width × the unhemmed fabric length.

3. Join the panels lengthwise, 1 side piece on each side of the center piece, and finish the seam allowance as desired.

4. Hem.

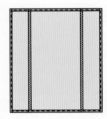

HEMMING OPTION 1

1. Make and press a ½˝ double-fold hem. (See Double-Fold Hem, page 29.)

2. Edgestitch the inside fold.

HEMMING OPTION 2

1. Make and press a ½˝ double-fold hem.

2. Unfold a corner.

3. Bring the tip of 1 corner in to meet the intersection of the innermost set of creases. Press the fold with the tip of an iron.

4. Make a 45° fold at the position of the tip. This will bring the creases on the right and wrong sides of the fold in line. Insert a pin through the center of the fold to secure.

5. Refold the hems on each side to make a mitered corner.

6. Repeat Steps 2–5 at each corner.

7. Edgestitch the inside fold.

Round Tablecloths

Standard round tablecloth sizes are either 70″ (for 44″–60″ tables) or 90″ (for 60″–78″ tables) in diameter. To make a custom round tablecloth, measure the table across the center to determine the diameter. Determine the drop length.

Table Diameter + (Drop × 2) = Desired Finished Diameter

Add in the hem allowance for a narrow rolled hem (see Rolled Hem, page 29) or single-fold bias binding (page 45). Wide hems are not recommended.

Desired Finished Diameter + (Hem Allowance × 2) = Unhemmed Diameter

1. Prepiece fabric to provide enough width (see Panel Sizing and Assembly, page 88) to cut a square slightly larger than the needed diameter.

2. Fold the square into fourths.

3. Tie the end of a piece of string to a fabric marker. Cut the string to half the desired finished diameter. Pin the cut end of the string to the folded corner.

4. Keeping the string evenly taut, draw an arc.

5. Cut through all the layers at the marking.

6. Finish with single-fold bias tape (see Applying Single-Fold Bias Tape, page 49) or a narrow rolled hem (see Hemming Curved Edges, page 31).

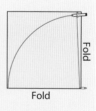

Napkins

Sizing is a matter of personal preference, but napkins are usually square with a finished size between 14″ × 14″ and 20″ × 20″. Determine the type of hem to be used and calculate the starting fabric size:

Desired Finished Width + (Hem Allowance × 2) = Unhemmed Fabric Width

Desired Finished Length + (Hem Allowance × 2) = Unhemmed Fabric Length

1. Cut the fabric to your calculated measurements.

2. Hem the edges as desired (see Hems, page 29). Mitered corners are an attractive, durable finish (see Hemming Option 2, page 89).

> **TIP**
> Choose fabrics that are machine washable. Synthetics and blends are more stain resistant than natural fibers.

Table Runners and Place Mats

The standard place mat is a 14″ × 18″ rectangle, but size and shape may vary. A table runner can be shorter than the table or hang over at the ends. The width usually ranges from 16″ to 24″. The ends can have squared or rounded corners, or a geometric or curved shape.

Squared corners   Rounded corners   Curved ends   Geometric ends

> **TIP**
> A roll of gift wrap is a helpful tool for determining table runner and/or place mat size and shape. "Audition" different variations on your table before cutting and sewing fabric. For rounded corners and ends, use dishes as tracing templates.

1. Cut the fabric to your calculated measurements and desired shape (see Napkins, above).

2. Finish the edges using one of the following options.

Hemmed Table Runner or Place Mats

Hem with mitered corners (see Hemming Option 2, page 89).

Frayed Table Runner or Place Mats

1. Determine the length of the desired "fringe." Make a line of stitching that distance from the edge on all sides.

2. Pull the threads at the raw edges to fray up to the stitching line.

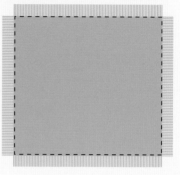

LINED TABLE RUNNER OR PLACE MATS

1. Cut a piece of backing fabric the same size as the top fabric.

2. Place right sides together and stitch around the edges, leaving a small opening for turning.

3. Trim the seam allowance around the corners.

4. Turn right side out and hand stitch the opening closed.

Hand stitch.

> **NOTE** For a padded and/or quilted runner, cut a piece of thin batting to size and place it on the wrong side of one of the fabric pieces prior to stitching.

BIAS-TAPE-BOUND TABLE RUNNER OR PLACE MATS

1. Cut a piece of backing fabric the same size as the top fabric.

2. With wrong sides together, stitch near the aligned edges.

3. Finish with double-fold bias tape. (See Applying Double-Fold Bias Tape, page 50 and Turning Square Corners with Bias Tape, page 51.)

Belts and Key Fobs

Belt Sizing

A belt should be at least 2˝ longer than the wearer's waist measurement (see Size Charts, pages 116–122). More length can be added for decorative purposes (or expansion opportunities). Include a hardware attachment allowance (usually ¾˝ to 1˝) in the length as well. Standard belt width is between ¾˝ and 1¼˝, but width can range from skinny (less than ¾˝) to wide (2˝–3˝). Key fobs are usually 15˝ long × 1˝ wide, but the length can be varied for different hand sizes.

Belt Hardware

Bar buckle
Traditional belt buckle with a movable tang that fits through holes in the other end of the belt (usually grommet holes in fabric belts).

Military buckle
Solid buckle with a clamping mechanism to hold the belt. A metal tip is often used to protect the free end.

Slide
Has a center bar for belt attachment. The belt end slides through one end, over the bar, and out the other end.

D-rings

A pair of D-rings are attached to one end of the belt. The other end is pulled up through both rings and reinserted between them.

Key fob

Consists of a clamp with an attached U-shaped ring. The clamp holds the ends of the fabric together to make a loop. It usually includes a key ring that clips onto the clamp end.

Belt Materials

Webbing

A strong woven material that is commonly used for belts. It can be used alone or trimmed with ribbon or fabric. Synthetic webbing ends can be sealed by passing them through a flame. The ends of cotton webbings should be treated with a fray blocker or edge finished with a sewing machine.

Belting

A rigid interlining material that is inserted into a presewn fabric tube.

Fusible interfacing

Commonly used to give needed thickness to fabric belts (see Interfacing, page 34).

Basic Fabric Belts

1. Purchase 2 D-rings or a slide that will accommodate the desired finished belt width.

2. Determine the desired finished belt length.

3. Cut a strip of heavyweight fusible interfacing that is 1˝ longer than the desired finished length and twice the desired finished width.

4. Cut a strip of fabric that is 1˝ longer and 1˝ wider than the interfacing.

5. Center the interfacing on the wrong side of the fabric, fusible side down, and press.

6. Fold the edges of the fabric over the interfacing and press.

7. Fold the belt in half lengthwise. Edgestitch on all 4 edges.

8. Insert an end of the belt into the hardware and make a 1˝ fold over the bar (or 2 D-rings). Stitch back and forth near the edge to secure.

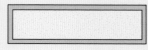

Basic Key Fobs

1. Purchase 1˝ fob hardware.

2. Cut a strip of heavyweight fusible interfacing 2˝ × 15˝.

3. Cut a strip of fabric 3˝ × 15˝.

4. Assemble. (See Steps 5–7 in Basic Fabric Belts, above.) Do not stitch or fold the short ends.

5. Bring the short ends together and hammer the hardware into place, enclosing the ends.

Bags

Types of Bags

Drawstring bag
Single piece of fabric with a casing at the top for a string- or ribbon-tied closure.

Sling (also called a hobo bag)
Soft and unstructured bag that is worn over the shoulder via a built-in strap.

Tote
Boxy, utilitarian bag with attached handles or straps.

Clutch
Small handheld bag without straps that closes with a zipper and/or flap.

Handbag (also called a purse)
Small- to medium-sized bag with handles and a zipper or snap closure. Handles or straps may be long enough to wear on the shoulder.

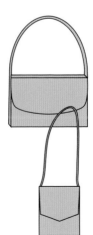

Messenger bag
Medium to large, but relatively short, bag with a flap and a long strap for wearing on the shoulder.

Crossbody bag
Small, narrow bag with a flap or zipper closure and a long strap for wearing on the shoulder opposite the bag.

Bag Fabrics

Most woven fabrics can be used for bag construction.

Canvas

Sturdy enough to be made into a bag without a lining or interfacing. It is also used as an interlining for thinner fabrics.

Oilcloth and laminated cotton

Sturdy as well as stain- and water-resistant. These fabrics can be lined with self-fabrics or combined with lighter-weight fabrics.

Quilter's cottons

Wide variety of colors and prints.
Soft totes and slings can be made using one or two layers of this fabric, but heavyweight interfacing or fusible fleece is a must for more structured bags.

Silks and satins

Elegant options for clutches and evening bags.

Interfacing

Bags are usually made from an outer fashion fabric and an inner lining. One or both fabrics may be fused to an interfacing (see Interfacing, page 34) to add structure and support. Another option is to add sew-in interfacing or additional fabric between the layers.

Straps

Either webbing or sewn fabric strips may be used for straps or handles (see Belt Materials, page 95). They can be attached between the fabric layers at the top seam or topstitched into place against the inner or outer fabric.

Optional Bag Hardware

Handles

Attached to the bag via loops or casings.
Available in a variety of shapes and materials.

Feet

Small metal "buttons" that add durability to
the bottom of a handbag or tote.

Rings and buckles

For strap attachment and/or
adjustment.

Bag Closures

MAGNETIC SNAPS

Magnetic snaps are a popular fastener for totes, clutches, and
messenger bags.

1. Mark the center snap position with a dot
on one of the bag pieces to be fastened.
Place the snap backing over the dot and use
it as a template to mark the slit positions.

2. If the fabric is not already fused to
interfacing, apply a square of heavyweight
fusible interfacing to the wrong side of the
fabric centered at the snap position.

3. Use a seam ripper
or sharp scissors to cut
the fabric at the slits.

4. From the right side, insert the
prongs in the closure through
the slits. Slip the backing over
the prongs on the
wrong side. Bend
the prongs over to
the sides to secure.

5. Repeat Steps 1-4 with the other snap half on the
second bag piece.

HOOK-AND-LOOP TAPE

Hook-and-loop tape makes a secure closure for bags with flaps.

1. Cut the tape to the desired length.

2. Before assembling the bag, sew the loop side of the tape to the exterior of the bag.

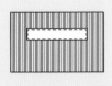

3. Sew the hook side of the tape to the right side of the flap lining (so that the stitching won't show on the completed bag).

4. Complete the bag assembly.

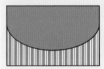

TIP

Glue or gluestick the tape in place before stitching. Using a heavy-duty needle, stitch all the way around the tape near the edges.

Adding a Zipper

Zippers can be used for top and pocket closures. Patterns for zippered bags usually contain installation instructions that are specific to the shape and style of bag. An open-topped lined bag can be modified to include a zipper using the following technique:

1. Purchase a separating zipper that is ½˝ to 1˝ shorter than the finished bag opening.

2. Cut 2 strips of fabric that are ½˝ longer than the zipper (stop to stop) and 2½˝ wide.

3. Fold the strips in half lengthwise, right sides together. Stitch ¼˝ from the raw edges, leaving a 1˝ opening in the center of the long edge.

4. For each strip, trim the seam allowance at the corners and turn right side out. Tuck the edges under at the opening and press.

5. Separate the zipper halves and lay them out with the working sides facing up.

6. Fold the top zipper seam allowances over to the back and pin into place. Apply glue to both zipper tapes.

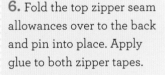

Apply glue to sides.

7. Stick the folded edges of the fabric strips to the tape close to the zipper teeth. Topstitch into place about ⅛˝ from the folded edge.

8. Place each strip/zipper assembly on the right side of a lining piece, working sides facing up, with the nonzipper edge ½˝ from the top seamline.

Lining

Edgestitch into place.

9. Assemble the bag as directed.

Making Darts

Darts are pointed tucks that give shape to a fitted garment.

1. Use a thick needle to pierce the pattern or template at the tip of the dart and the bottom of each dart leg.

2. Align the pattern or template with the wrong side of the fabric and use a fine washable marker or chalk pencil to mark the fabric through the holes.

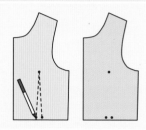

3. Connect the dots.

> **TIP**
> Another option is to use tracing paper and a tracing wheel to transfer the dart lines to the fabric.

NOTE It is helpful to draw an additional line that vertically bisects the dart. For triangle-shaped darts, draw the line from the dart point to the edge of the fabric. For diamond-shaped darts, draw the line from point to point.

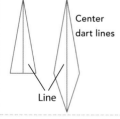

Center dart lines

Line

4. Fold the fabric, right sides together, along the center dart line. Align the dart markings on the sides. Secure with pins and/or press.

5. Stitch from one end of the dart marking to the other. Tie off the threads, or backstitch, at the beginning and end of the stitching.

6. Press the dart over to one side (generally toward the center front or center back of a garment).

Adding Facings

Facings are used as a means of edge finishing and giving structure to openings in a garment. The inner facing edge is identical to that of the garment. The outer edge is shaped to fit the inside of the garment. Facings are generally fused to an interfacing before sewing. In order to reduce bulk in the seam allowances of thicker fabrics, you may choose not to extend the interfacing all the way to the edges. The outer facing edge is usually finished with a serger overlock stitch, zigzag stitch, or narrow hem before the facing is attached to the garment.

1. Place the facing against the outer garment, right sides together.

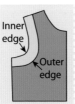

Inner edge
Outer edge

2. Stitch together using the specified seam allowance. Trim and/or snip curves.

3. Turn the facing to the wrong side of the garment and work the edge to fully roll out the seams. Press the edge so the facing is not visible on the right side of the garment.

4. Stitch through all the layers close to the inner or outer edge of the facing, or tack the edges of the facings at the seams to prevent shifting.

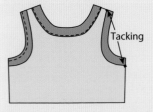

Tacking

NOTE Facings can be placed on the outside of the garment as a design detail. Fold under the seam allowance on the outside edge of the facing, and press. Stitch the right side of the facing to the wrong side of the garment. Turn the facing to the right side and edgestitch the pressed hem allowance into place.

Linings

Linings give a clean edge finish and add an extra layer to the garment. This not only hides and protects the garment's seams but also gives the extra opacity and drape that a slip would provide. In many cases, linings can be sewn from the same pattern pieces as the outer garment.

1. Construct the garment and lining separately, including darts and side seams.

2. Place the layers right sides together and sew at some (but not all) of the openings. In a sleeveless dress, for example, stitch the arm and neck openings but leave the back opening and bottom edges open.

3. Turn right side out through one of the unstitched areas. Complete the remaining seams. Hem the outer garment and lining separately to allow for movement.

> **TIP**
> Garments with facings can be modified to be lined, and vice versa.

Sewing Casings

Casings are channels that accommodate elastic. Most casings are made in a simliar fashion to hems (see Hems, page 29). The width of the casing should be about ⅛″ greater than the width of the elastic.

1. Finish the raw edge with a narrow fold.

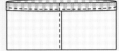

2. Fold the casing to the desired width and stitch, leaving an opening (usually at the center back) for elastic insertion.

3. Using a safety pin or a tool called a bodkin, feed the elastic through the casing.

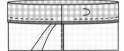

4. Overlap or butt the elastic's ends and then stitch securely.

5. Tuck the joined ends into the casing and stitch the opening closed. Spread the gathers evenly. Stitch back and forth over the casing at one or more seams to prevent twisting.

TIP

Single-fold bias tape (see Bias Tape, page 45) can be used to add a casing to a place on the garment that isn't on a folded edge (such as the waist of a dress or the middle of a sleeve). Be sure the distance between the two rows of stitching used to attach the binding is ⅛″ greater than the width of the elastic.

Sewing Set-In Sleeves

Adding sleeves to a garment utilizes the principles of curved piecing (see Curved Seams, page 24). The top of the sleeve (called the cap) is larger than the segment of the armhole to which it is attached. This is called cap ease, and it allows the sleeve to move and hang properly. To accommodate the cap ease, the pieces should be aligned and pinned at regular intervals.

Flat Sleeve Attachment

This technique allows for more working room and easier sewing.

> **NOTE** Sew the front and back bodice pieces together at the shoulder seams. Leave the side seams of the bodice open.

1. With right sides together, match the center of the sleeve with the center of the armhole, and pin.

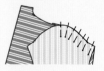

2. Match the corner of the sleeve with the corresponding end of the armhole, and pin.

3. Align and pin the edges in between.

4. Repeat on the other side of the center point.

5. Stitch the armhole seam and edge finish as desired.

6. Bring the front and back bodice pieces together. Align the sleeve and bodice side seam edges. Stitch and edge finish as desired.

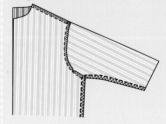

Tubular Sleeve Attachment

In this more advanced technique, the side seams are completed before attaching the sleeve.

1. Stitch and edge finish the sleeve underarm seams, the bodice side seams, and the bodice shoulder seams.

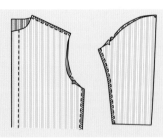

2. Turn the sleeve so the right side is facing out. Place the sleeve inside the bodice, right sides facing each other. Match the bodice side seam to the sleeve underarm seam, and pin. Match the bodice shoulder seam to the sleeve shoulder point, and pin.

3. Align and pin the edges in between.

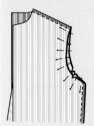

4. Stitch the armhole seam and edge finish as desired.

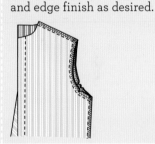

5. Pull the sleeve out and away from the bodice.

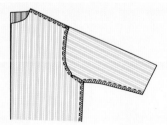

Patterns

Selecting Patterns

Not long ago, shopping for patterns involved flipping through large pattern catalogs in fabric stores. Now, the Internet has made pattern shopping more efficient and informative.

Major pattern companies such as Vogue, McCall's, Butterick, and New Look provide catalogs online and offer search features that allow for quick selection by specific style. The patterns can then be purchased from a store or ordered from the website. Many patterns are available as electronic downloads that are printed at home on 8½˝ × 11˝ paper and assembled into full-sized patterns. Independent pattern-makers are gaining market share thanks to favorable reviews on social networking sites and blogs. Websites such as patternreview.com, burdastyle.com, craftsy.com, and others have created communities for sewists of all levels to share their experiences with both independent and commercial patterns.

Consider the following factors when selecting a pattern.

Sizing

Depending on the company, pattern sizes may vary greatly from off-the-rack sizes. Patterns often include multiple sizes rather than a single size. Be sure to select the appropriate size (see Verifying Sizing, page 109) and select the package that includes your size. Internet reviews are a good way to find out if a pattern runs true to size.

Difficulty Level

Patterns may be labeled with a needed skill level. Unless they are marked as easy or for beginners, many patterns assume an intermediate level of experience. Those with clear and detailed instructions give beginners a better chance for success. Again, Internet reviews can give insight into both the skills needed and the quality of the instructions.

Material Requirements

Be sure that the item can be made from a fabric that you are comfortable sewing, laundering or dry-cleaning, and wearing. Also keep yardage requirements and cost in mind.

Verifying Sizing

Pattern companies usually provide size charts in pattern books, online, and within the patterns themselves. Compare your measurements to the chart and select the size that is closest to your own. If one measurement falls into a different size bracket, you may need to modify the pattern (see Adjusting for Height, page 113, and Adjusting for Girth, page 115). Patterns often provide finished garment measurements. If they do not, it is a good idea to calculate the finished measurements at specific points (such as the bustline and hips). (See Calculating Pattern Finished Measurements, page 112.) Compare the garment measurements to those of a nice-fitting garment that you already own. Or you can subtract your body measurements from the garment measurements to determine how much ease is included in the pattern. This will help you predict the fit of the garment (see Ease, page 112).

Pattern Abbreviations and Markings

Pattern pieces often have placement and stitching information printed on them. Because of space constraints, the following abbreviations are sometimes used:

RS (right side), **RST** (right sides together), **RSO** (right sides out)

WS (wrong side), **WST** (wrong sides together), **WSO** (wrong sides out)

SA (seam allowance), **CF** (center front), **CB** (center back)

△ Notch
Indicates a matching point for accurately joining two pieces. May be cut into the seam allowance or extended beyond the raw edge.

● Dot
Indicates a stitching stop, matching point, or placement point for objects such as buttons.

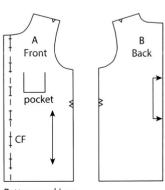

Pattern markings

Buttonhole placement Indicates position of buttonholes and buttons. Placement is usually represented by a straight line or "I"-shaped mark. An X represents the button position.

Placement lines Indicate position for pockets or decorative elements.

Double-pointed arrow

 Indicates how the pattern piece should be placed relative to the grain of the fabric.

Bent double-pointed arrow

Indicates that an edge of the pattern should be placed on a fabric fold.

The outer edges of the pattern are usually cutting lines, unless the seam allowance is not included (common in European patterns). In multisized nested pattern sets, the cutting lines may have different thicknesses, dashing patterns, or colors for different sizes. Other lines (for example, stitching, hem position, or pocket placement) are usually defined by text on the pattern.

Cutting layouts show the ideal placement of pattern pieces on the fabric. If the cutting layout is not followed, a fabric shortage may occur. Folds are sometimes represented by dashed lines. Pieces placed on the fold line will be doubled. Pieces placed on folded fabric (but set apart) will be mirror images of one another. Selvages are marked to indicate the orientation of the fabric.

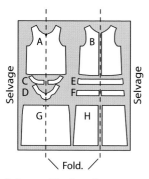

Pattern cutting layout

Body Measurements

Obtaining accurate measurements is the first step in constructing a great-fitting garment. For most articles of clothing, the pattern size is chosen based on one or more of only three horizontal body measurements: bust/chest, waist, and hips. For the best results, take measurements over the undergarments that will be worn with the finished garment.

Bust/Chest

Measure around the breasts or chest at the fullest point.

Waist

Measure at the narrowest point. You can find this point by bending over to the side and locating the crease that forms at the side.

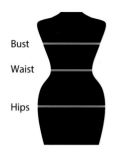

Bust

Waist

Hips

Hips

Measure around the hips at the fullest point.

Compare the measurements to those in the size chart that goes with the pattern. Depending on the wearer's proportions, all parts of the body may not fall into the same size category. Base your pattern selection on the measurements that are most relevant to the garment you are making. Also note whether or not parts of the garment have a free fit. For example, pajama pants usually have a stretch elastic waistband, so the hip measurement is most important. For a fitted garment such as a sheath dress, all three measurements are important. A general rule of thumb is to choose the size dictated by the largest measurement. Alter the remaining parts of the pattern (see Adjusting for Girth, page 115) or take in the garment during the sewing process.

Vertical measurements are helpful for deciding how long to make different parts of the garment and whether or not a pattern should be modified for the wearer's height (see Adjusting for Height, page 113).

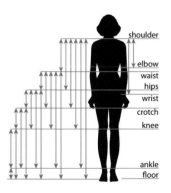

shoulder

elbow
waist
hips
wrist
crotch
knee

ankle
floor

NOTE Over the years, retail sizing has deviated from the original garment standards for women's clothing. Your store-bought size may be vastly different from your pattern size. For example, a woman with 38″ hips would wear a size 6 off the rack but would need a size 12 pattern to make a properly fitting garment. Some companies have developed pattern lines that are more consistent with current retail sizing, but it is always best to base your pattern selection on measurements rather than a specific size.

Ease

Ease is the difference between the garment measurements and the body measurements. If a garment were made with no ease, it would be skintight. *Wearing ease* is the absolute minimum amount of ease needed for movement and comfort. Different parts of the body require different amounts of ease. *Design ease* is anything beyond wearing ease that gives the garment a specific fit or style. For example, a dress that is semifitted in the bust and very loose-fitting in the hips would be an A-line style.

WEARING EASE					
	CLOSE-FITTING	FITTED	SEMI-FITTED	LOOSE-FITTING	VERY LOOSE-FITTING
Bust	2⅞″	3″–4″	4⅛″–5″	5⅛″–8″	More than 8″
Waist	1″	1⅛″–2″	2⅛″–3″	3⅛″–4″	More than 4″
Hips	1⅞″	2″–3″	3⅛″–4″	4⅛″–6″	More than 6″

NOTE The ranges for wearing ease apply to garments made from woven fabrics. Since knit fabrics stretch, knit garments can be made with very little (or even negative) ease and still fit comfortably.

Calculating Pattern Finished Measurements

Measure the pattern pieces at the desired line—generally bustline, waistline, or hipline. Add the front and back measurements (remember to double the measurement if the piece is placed on a fold) and then subtract the seam allowances. For patterns with darts, exclude the darts from your measurements. This will give you the finished measurement at the selected line.

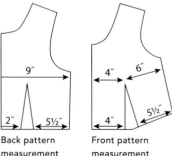

Back pattern measurement

Front pattern measurement

Adjusting for Height

Most patterns are designed to fit a specific height range. For women, this is 5´5˝–5´6˝; for men, 5´10˝; and for children, the average height for the given age or size (see Size Charts, pages 116–122). For misses' and women's sizes, some patterns are available for petites, but not for tall women. For children and men, there are no separate patterns for slims, huskies, talls, or shorts. Within a pattern set there is some vertical variation for the different sizes—the smaller sizes are slightly shorter, and the larger sizes are slightly longer. For the most part, however, adjustments for height must be made by the sewist.

For most free-fitting garments, adjusting the pattern for height is simply a matter of adding or subtracting length at the bottom edge. For more fitted garments, especially pants and dresses, modifications to accommodate different proportions must be made at one or more points between the top edge and the bottom edge of the pattern. Many patterns include double lines that are labeled "lengthen or shorten here." For tops, this marking is usually between the bustline and the waistline. For pants and skirts, it may be between the waist and the crotch, between the crotch and the knee, or both. If lines are not shown, you can add them.

NOTE You must make height adjustments on the pattern, prior to cutting the fabric.

To shorten a pattern: Cut at the double lines. Overlap the pattern pieces the necessary amount and tape together. Blend the dart and side lines to reconnect them.

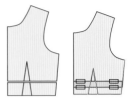

To lengthen a pattern: Cut at the double lines. Place the pattern pieces on a separate sheet of paper, the necessary distance apart, and tape together. Reconnect the dart and side lines. Cut the paper flush with the pattern edges.

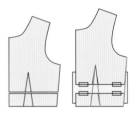

Vertical-measurement charts are very useful for determining if and where adjustments should be made. For example, say a knee-length dress is designed for a woman with a height of 5´6˝, but the wearer is 5´10˝. The vertical-length charts show that the shoulder-to-knee measurement is 38¾˝ for 5´6˝ and 41½˝ for 5´10˝—a 2¾˝ difference.

In addition, the shoulder-to-waist measurements for the pattern and wearer differ by 1˝, and the waist-to-knee measurements differ by 1¾˝. To give even more detail, the waist-to-crotch measurements differ by 1¼˝, and the crotch-to-knee measurements by ½˝. In order to fit a 5´10˝ woman, the pattern should be lengthened 1˝ between the shoulder and waist, 1¼˝ between the waist and crotch, and ½˝ between the crotch and knee.

Adjusting for Girth

Patterns are usually designed to fit a standard set of proportions. Most misses' size patterns are designed for a relatively balanced hipline and bustline and a significantly smaller waist. For women's sizes, the bustline and waistline are about the same, and the hipline is larger.

Actual figures vary widely in proportions. The good news is that most patterns can be adjusted to fit almost any figure type. Cutting lines can be moved out to make a portion of the garment larger, or moved in to make it smaller. Openings such as necklines and armholes can be increased or decreased as well. When adjusting patterns, it is a good idea to make a test garment out of inexpensive fabric so that the fit can be fine-tuned.

The waistline is one of the easiest parts of a pattern to adjust. It can be increased by moving the side seams out and/or decreasing the dart width (a). It can be taken in by moving the side seams in and/or increasing the dart width (b).

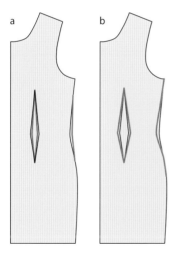

Patterns can also be merged to get the best possible fit. For example, if the wearer measures a size 8 in the bust and a size 10 in the hips, the top part of a fitted dress pattern could be traced from the size 8 and the bottom from a size 10, and the lines blended at the waistline.

~ Size Charts ~

AGE SIZE	0M	3M	6M	12M	18M	24M 2	36M 3	4	5	6	6X
INFANTS', TODDLERS', AND LITTLE KIDS' STANDARD SIZES (in inches)											
CHEST	16	17	18	19	20	21	22	23	24	25	25½
WAIST	-	-	-	-	-	20½	21	21½	22	22½	23
HIP	-	-	-	-	-	21½	22½	23½	24½	25½	26½
HEIGHT	22	24	26½	29	31	34	37	40	43	46	48

Note: Children can be difficult to measure. In babies, the chest, waist, and hip run about the same, so the chest is the only measuring point needed. For toddlers, the hip measurement should be taken over diapers, if applicable.

If the child is between sizes, always choose the larger size to accommodate rapid growth.

HEIGHT (Age in Months)	24″ (3M)	26½″ (6M)	29″ (12M)	31″ (18M)	34″ (24M)	37″ (36M)
INFANTS' AND TODDLERS' VERTICAL MEASUREMENTS (in inches)						
Shoulder to wrist	8	8¾	10	10½	11¼	12¼
Shoulder to elbow	4¾	5¼	5¾	6	6½	6½
Shoulder to waist	6¼	7	7½	7¾	8¼	8½
Shoulder to hip	8¾	10	10½	11¼	12¼	13
Shoulder to crotch	10½	11½	12½	13	14¼	15¼
Shoulder to knee	13	14½	16¼	17½	19	20½
Shoulder to ankle	17	19¼	21½	23½	25¾	28
Shoulder to floor	18¼	20½	23	25	27½	29¾
Waist to crotch	4¼	4½	5	5¼	6	6¾
Waist to knee	6¾	7½	8¾	9¾	10¾	12
Waist to ankle	10¾	12¼	14	15¾	17½	19½
Waist to floor	12	13½	15½	17¼	19¼	21¼
Hip to floor	9½	10½	12½	13¾	15¼	16¾
Crotch to knee	2½	3	3¾	4½	4¾	5¼
Crotch to ankle	6½	7¾	9	10½	11½	12¾
Crotch to floor	7¾	9	10½	12	13¼	14½
Knee to floor	5¼	6	6¾	7½	8½	9¼
Ankle to floor	1¼	1¼	1½	1½	1¾	1¾

Note: Children's sizing is based on averages for different ages, but measurements are much more important than age for determining size. Like adults, children vary in height and proportion. Average heights are provided with the measurements above. Tall, thin children may have measurements that indicate a very small pattern size. In this case it is usually better to choose the size indicated by the height measurement so that the proportions are correct.

LITTLE KIDS' VERTICAL MEASUREMENTS (in inches)				
HEIGHT (Age/Size)	40″ (4)	43″ (5)	46″ (6)	48″ (6X)
Shoulder to wrist	12¾	13½	14¼	15¼
Shoulder to elbow	7	7½	8	8¾
Shoulder to waist	8¾	9½	10¼	10½
Shoulder to hip	13½	14½	15¾	16¼
Shoulder to crotch	16	17¼	18½	18¾
Shoulder to knee	22	24	25¾	27
Shoulder to ankle	30½	33¼	36	37½
Shoulder to floor	32½	35½	38¼	40
Waist to crotch	7¼	7¾	8¼	8¼
Waist to knee	13¼	14½	15½	16½
Waist to ankle	21¾	23¾	25¾	27
Waist to floor	23¾	26	28	29½
Hip to floor	19	21	22½	23¾
Crotch to knee	6	6¾	7¼	8¼
Crotch to ankle	14½	16	17½	18¾
Crotch to floor	16½	18¼	19¾	21¼
Knee to floor	10½	11½	12½	13
Ankle to floor	2	2¼	2¼	2¼

GIRLS' SIZES (in inches)

	7	8	10	12	14	16
Chest	26	27	28½	30	31½	33
Waist	22½	23	24	25	26	27
Hips	27½	28½	30	32	34	36
Height	51	53	55	57½	60	62½

BOYS' SIZES (in inches)

	7	8	10	12	14	16
Chest	25¼	26½	28	29½	31½	33
Waist	23	23½	24½	25½	26½	27½
Hips	25¾	26½	28	30	32	34
Height	48	50	54	58	60	64

NOTE Girls' and boys' sizing deviates starting at size 7 as girls develop a smaller waist-to-hip ratio.

There is some overlap between teen and misses' sizing in hip size, but misses' sizes are associated with smaller waist and larger bust measurements.

GIRLS' AND BOYS' VERTICAL MEASUREMENTS (in inches)

HEIGHT	4′0″ (48″)	4′2″ (50″)	4′4″ (52″)	4′6″ (54″)	4′8″ (56″)	4′10″ (58″)	5′0″ (60″)
Shoulder to wrist	17	18	18½	19½	20	20½	21½
Shoulder to elbow	10	10½	11	11¼	11¾	12	12½
Shoulder to waist	10½	10½	11¼	11¼	11¾	12	12¼
Shoulder to hip	16½	16½	17¼	17¾	18¼	19	19¼
Shoulder to crotch	19	19¼	20¼	20½	21¼	21¾	22¼
Shoulder to knee	27	28	29½	30½	32	33	33¾
Shoulder to ankle	37¾	39¼	41¼	42¾	44¾	46½	47¾
Shoulder to floor	40	41½	43½	45¼	47¼	49	50¼
Waist to crotch	8½	8¾	9	9¼	9½	9¾	10
Waist to knee	16½	17½	18¼	19¼	20¼	21	21½
Waist to ankle	27¼	28¾	30	31½	33	34½	35½
Waist to floor	29½	31	32¼	34	35½	37	38
Hip to floor	23½	25	26¼	27½	29	30	31
Crotch to knee	8	8¾	9¼	10	10¾	11¼	11½
Crotch to ankle	18¾	20	21	22¼	23½	24¾	25½
Crotch to floor	21	22¼	23¼	24¾	26	27¼	28
Knee to floor	13	13½	14	14¾	15¼	16	16½
Ankle to floor	2¼	2¼	2¼	2½	2½	2½	2½

For heights outside the chart range, consult the adult size charts.

MISSES' SIZES (in inches)

	*	2	4	6	8	10	12	14	16	18	20	22	24
BUST P	-	28½	29½	30½	31½	33	35	37	39	41	43	45
BUST R	33	34	35	36	37	38½	40½	42	44	46½	-	-
WAIST P	-	22	23	24	25	26½	28	30	32	34	37	39
WAIST R	26	27	28	29	30	31½	33	35	38	40	-	-
HIPS P	-	31½	32½	33½	34½	36	38	40	42	44	46	48
HIPS R	36	37	38	39	40	41½	43	45	47	49½	-	-

P = Pattern; R = Ready-to-Wear

WOMEN'S SIZES (in inches)

	*	16W	18W	20W	22W	24W	26W	28W	30W
BUST P	38	40	42	44	46	48	50	52
BUST R	44	46	48	50	52	54	56	58
WAIST P	31	33	35	37	39	41½	44	46½
WAIST R	38	40	41	44	46	48	50	52
HIPS P	42	44	46	48	50	52	54	56
HIPS R	46	48	50	52	54	56	58	60

P = Pattern; R = Ready-to-Wear

NOTE Misses' and women's size charts were constructed based on the size charts of major pattern companies and several major clothing retailers. The remaining size and vertical-measurements charts were derived from public standards.

MISSES' AND WOMEN'S VERTICAL MEASUREMENTS (in inches)

HEIGHT	5'0" (60")	5'2" (62")	5'4" (64")	5'6" (66")	5'8" (68")	5'10" (70")	6'0" (72")
Shoulder to wrist	21½	22¼	23¼	24	24¾	25½	26¼
Shoulder to elbow	12½	13	13½	13¾	14¼	14¾	15¼
Shoulder to waist	13	14¼	15	15½	16	16½	17
Shoulder to hip	20	21¾	23	24¼	24¾	26¼	27¾
Shoulder to crotch	23	24½	26¼	27¼	28	29½	31
Shoulder to knee	34½	36	37¾	38¾	40	41½	43
Shoulder to ankle	48½	50	52¼	53¾	56¼	58	60
Shoulder to floor	51	52¾	55	56½	59	61	63
Waist to crotch	10	10¼	11¼	11¾	12	13	14
Waist to knee	21½	21¾	22¾	23¼	24	25	26
Waist to ankle	35½	35¾	37¼	38¼	40¼	41½	43
Waist to floor	38	38½	40	41	43	44½	46
Hip to floor	31	31	32	32¼	34¼	34¾	35¼
Crotch to knee	11½	11½	11½	11½	12	12	12
Crotch to ankle	25½	25½	26	26½	28¼	28½	29
Crotch to floor	28	28¼	28¾	29¼	31	31½	32
Knee to floor	16½	16¾	17¼	17¾	19	19½	20
Ankle to floor	2½	2¾	2¾	2¾	2¾	3	3

MEN'S SIZES (in inches)

	34	36	38	40	42	44	46	48	50	52	54	56
Chest	34	36	38	40	42	44	46	48	50	52	54	56
Waist	28	30	32	34	36	39	42	44	46	48	50	52
Hips	35	37	39	41	43	45	47	49	51	53	55	57

Note: *In many adult males, the waist is larger than the chest or hips and the natural waistline may be difficult to locate. When sizing, keep in mind that men's pants are often worn at the hips.*

MEN'S VERTICAL MEASUREMENTS (IN INCHES)

HEIGHT	5'4" (64")	5'6" (66")	5'8" (68")	5'10" (70")	6'0" (72")	6'2" (74")	6'4" (76")
Shoulder to wrist	23¼	24	24¾	25½	26¼	27	27¾
Shoulder to elbow	13¾	14	14½	15	15¼	15¼	16¼
Shoulder to waist	14½	15	15	15½	15¾	16½	17¼
Shoulder to hip	22	22½	23	24	24½	25½	26¼
Shoulder to crotch	25¼	26¼	26½	27½	28	29¼	30¼
Shoulder to knee	37½	38½	39½	40½	42	43¼	44½
Shoulder to ankle	52½	53¾	55½	57¼	58¾	60¾	62½
Shoulder to floor	55¼	56½	58¼	60	61¾	63¾	65½
Waist to crotch	10¾	11¼	11½	12	12¼	12¾	13
Waist to knee	23	23½	24½	25	26¼	26¾	27¼
Waist to ankle	38	38¾	40½	41¾	43	44¼	45¼
Waist to floor	40¾	41½	43¼	44½	46	47¼	48¼
Hip to floor	33¼	34	35¼	36	37¼	38¼	39¼
Crotch to knee	12¼	12¼	13	13	14	14	14¼
Crotch to ankle	27¼	27½	29	29¾	30¾	31½	32¼
Crotch to floor	30	30¼	31¾	32½	33¾	34½	35¼
Knee to floor	17¾	18	18¾	19½	19¾	20½	21
Ankle to floor	2¾	2¾	2¾	2¾	3	3	3

~ Number Conversions ~

DECIMALS TO FRACTIONS

Decimal	Fraction
.125	⅛
.25	¼
.333	⅓
.375	⅜
.5	½
.625	⅝
.667	⅔
.75	¾
.875	⅞

YARDS TO INCHES TO DECIMALS

Yards	Inches	Decimals
⅛	4½	.125
¼	9	.25
⅓	12	.333
⅜	13½	.375
½	18	.50
⅝	22½	.625
⅔	24	.667
¾	27	.75
⅞	31½	.875
1	36	1.00

YARDS TO CENTIMETERS/METERS

Yards	Centimeters/Meters
⅛	11.5cm
¼	23cm
⅜	34cm
½	45.5cm
⅝	57cm
¾	68.5cm
⅞	80cm
1	91.5cm
1⅛	1.05m
1¼	1.15m
1⅜	1.25m
1½	1.35m
1⅝	1.5m
1¾	1.6m
1⅞	1.7 m
2	1.85m
2⅛	1.95m
2¼	2m
2⅜	2.15m
2½	2.3m
2⅝	2.4m
2¾	2.5m
2⅞	2.65m

~Index~

About the Author

CARLA HEGEMAN CRIM, founder of Scientific Seamstress LLC, is a molecular biologist turned patternmaker. She has a B.S. in biology from Virginia Commonwealth University and a Ph.D. in plant physiology from Virginia Tech and was a postdoctoral fellow at Cornell University. She is a self-taught seamstress who has been experimenting with fabric for more than 30 years. The Scientific Seamstress blog and pattern series are well known for their complete, easy-to-follow instructions and detailed illustrations. When her son came along, she decided to stay home with him and build a business out of sewing. For the first few years, she focused on elaborate clothing designs for dolls and children. She had many requests for her patterns and began publishing them in 2006. Carla also collaborates with popular fabric designer Jennifer Paganelli on a series of Sis Boom patterns for children and adults. Her first book, *Sewn Hats*, was published in 2013. When she isn't in her sewing lab, Carla enjoys gardening, yoga, and spending time with her family.

31192020564603

Essential Sewing Reference Tool